Eight simple steps to building trust and business from private clients

Uncovering the secrets of Winning Business from Private Clients

Invaluable insights on working for ultra-high net worth clients and their family offices

By Caroline Garnham

BConnect Limited and Garnham Family Office Services
in association with

Filament Publishing Ltd
16, Croydon Road, Waddon, Croydon,
Surrey, CRO 4PA, United Kingdom
Telephone +44 (0)20 8688 2598
Fax +44 (0)20 7183 7186
info@filamentpublishing.com
www.filamentpublishing.com

ISBN 978-1-912256-49-5

Printed by IngramSpark

Disclaimer

The information contained in this publication is intended solely to
provide general guidance on matters of interest for the personal use of
the reader, who accepts full responsibility for its use. The application
and impact of laws can vary widely based on the specific facts involved.
Accordingly, the information contained in this book is provided with the
understanding that the authors and publishers are not herein engaged
in rendering legal, accounting, tax, or other professional advice or
services. As such, it should not be used as a substitute for consultation
with professional accounting, tax, legal or other competent advisers.
Before making any decision or taking any action, you should consult a
qualified professional.

About the author

Caroline Garnham, a former leading private client lawyer and head of Simmons & Simmons private client practice for fifteen years, was nominated as one of the top five leading private client lawyers by *The Lawyer* in 2011. She was a contributor for the *Financial Times* from 1986 to 1998, pioneered the area of law now known as Family Governance and proposed and drafted the Executive Entity Act for the Bahamas, which became law in December 2011.

This book draws on her extensive knowledge and intimate experience in working for some of the world's wealthiest families. Pulling together scores of examples, she looks at the relationship of the UHNW community and their advisors from both perspectives. She believes that by understanding each other, they can work together more productively.

Caroline had a break from practicing law in December 2011 to focus her attention on making investment opportunities, exclusive luxury products and relevant information more available to the UHNW community.

She designed a digital platform which she now runs as a joint venture enterprise **www.bconnectclub.com**. It provides a safe and secure neutral website, where UHNWIs can find investment opportunities, luxury products and services and where subscribers can promote their case studies, news and views to this hard to reach market.

Caroline is actively advising clients. She is passionate about the need for UHNW families to use teams of trusted advisers *on a regular basis.* They cannot hope to know the detail of what risks lie in wait for them and need a team of advisers – which she calls a 'Ring of Confidence' – to keep them fully informed.

If you are an advisor to Private Clients and want to find out more about building a Ring of Confidence for your clients sign up to receive Caroline's weekly blog, *Note from Caroline* it's FREE. Simply go to http://www.garnhamfos.com/notes-from-caroline

And if you would like to know more about how you can promote your investments, products, or news and views to the BConnect Club of UHNW members, go to **www.bconnectclub.com**.

Contents

Foreword

Trust: the basis of the successful UHNW client and advisor relationship

Chapter summary:

- UHNWs need advisors they can trust.

- They are tired of being fleeced and want to be treated as human beings, not ATMs.

- How you can build client relationships based on trust while also saving time and money.

Working as a private client lawyer for more than twenty five years, I know how hard it is to win new business from private clients. So when I took a break from private practice as a lawyer for many of the world's super rich, I wanted to find out what they wanted from their investments, luxury product providers and professional advisors and how to make it easier for them to get what they want.

The super rich may not have misgivings about a mortgage or where the next meal is coming from, but they do have their own worries, which need to be understood and served. This community contributes significantly in taxes which benefits us all. In Great Britain, the top 1% pay 30% of our income tax, they spend in our shops and oil the wheels of our economy – and yet in general they are poorly served and often despised.

This book, *Uncovering the secrets to winning business from private clients*, is designed to help advisors understand the super rich and to show them how they can give their clients what they need in order to manage their wealth and lives in the manner they want.

To win business from private clients, is not Garnham homespun it is based on years of research into the numerous scientific examples of human behavior, simply applied to the private client industry. It is much easier and cheaper to win business than you could imagine, but to be successful, you may need rethink how to go about it.

UHNWs are fed up with being fleeced

George, a PR agent, who acts for one of the wealthiest people in the *Sunday Times* Rich List, arranged to meet his client in a country golf club. George arrived at the agreed time, but still hovering above him was his client's helicopter and it wasn't making an approach to land. George phoned him to find out why. The client was refusing to land due to a charge of £95. George offered to pay – he hadn't spent two hours travelling to a far-flung golf club only to have the meeting cancelled. The client – in a rage – refused to let him pay. This was a matter of principle. So George had to plead with the golf club to waive its fee, which it did, and George's client finally landed.

Of course, the client could have paid the fee, or George could've paid it, but that was not the point. The client wanted to know why it cost £95 to land a helicopter and yet it was free to park a car!

Surely the golf club should be encouraging their members to arrive by helicopter as it added cachet to the club. By charging a fee, the club was in severe danger of losing one of their most prestigious members purely through greed. Their thinking was if you can afford a helicopter you can

afford a landing fee. It's like saying if you drive to the club in a Bentley you pay a parking fee, but if you arrive in a Toyota you don't.

UHNW individuals are being fingered for money ALL THE TIME. It is hardly surprising therefore that they fly off the handle and appear difficult when they are being fleeced for yet more cash. Being pestered for money is a way of life for them and most of them hate it, which is why they want to preserve their privacy.

We may watch their antics with surprise, but most of us do not know what it is like to be wealthy. However, as advisors, we need to understand them.

They are looking for people they can trust. But trustworthy people cannot be bought with money because this precious quality is an attitude rather than a product. UHNWs want advisors who care for them, who see them as people rather than money-mountains.

What do UHNWs really want?

- To build a relevant team of trusted advisers – a Ring of Confidence which advises them on a regular basis

- Confidence that their advisors are acting in their best interests

- To preserve their privacy as they seek out investment opportunities, luxury products and services and relevant information on how to manage their assets. A platform like **www.bconnectclub.com** allows them to find what they need while retaining their privacy.

- To avoid making mistakes. They want to learn from you about how to manage their wealth, find luxury products and services and enjoy themselves without revealing who they are or in what they may be interested.

- Convenience. They want to find everything they need to know about spending, investing and giving wealth in one place at, one time.

Can you build trust with clients while saving time and money?

Advisors to the UHNW community have been squeezed. Since 2008 they have been fined $320 billion dollars for criminal conspiracy; advising their clients how legitimately to avoid taxes. They have been silenced. This does not mean the UHNW community, if fully tax compliant, cannot plan to protect their privacy or their assets from opportunistic governments, disgruntled colleagues, former spouses, remote family members or greedy creditors.

Advisors now need to find new ways to win business and to serve their clients' best interests. They need to embrace digital technology, understand how to win business from 'private clients' as well as how to save time and money.

This book aims to challenge existing ways of doing business, since the old model is not working.

This book is split into eight chapters:

- Setting goals

- Planning

- Time management

- Getting there

- Getting more

- Delivery

- Retain and maintain, and

- Trust

In each chapter the book challenges the advisor to understand their clients and to give them what they want, by looking after their clients' best interests, building trust and winning new business.

To get you started, sign up to Caroline's weekly blog, it's FREE. Simply go to **www.garnhamfos.com/notes-from-caroline** and give us your name and contact details.

Then you can sign up to our Books Extras – training material on how you can put into practice, easily and simply what is contained in the

Chapter. If you want to sign up for all eight you will get one FREE, just click on the QR code below , or go to the following link:

https://garnhamfos.squarespace.com/wbfpc-extras/chapters-1-8-training-materials

If you would like to know more about how you can promote your products and services to our UHNW members on BConnect Club, simply click on the QR code below, or go to the following link:

www.bconnectclub.com

Chapter 1
Goal setting for advisors

Chapter summary:

- Why advisors need to embrace their client-facing role.

- Pay attention to late payments.

- How well do you know your clients?

- Tools for advisors: setting SMART goals.

- Tools for advisors: the vision statement.

Professional advisors

Many advisors define themselves by the work they do. Very few would label themselves as business people; their up-to-date knowledge and experience sets them apart. They see themselves as experts.

> Because advisors do not see themselves as business people, they will never have the enjoyment and profitability they deserve. They need to readjust their thinking.

Sally, a professional trustee, lives in Guernsey and is a member of the Society of Trusts and Estate Practitioners. She goes to at least seven conferences a year to make sure she is up-to-date with the latest cases and current thinking. She has more than twenty big clients, but finds them tricky to deal with: they are always complaining about her fees and trying to negotiate them down. Secretly, she would prefer her job if it didn't involve clients. She sees herself as a professional, and is proud of being such. Sally does not see herself as a businesswoman. If she had wanted to go into business, she wouldn't have spent so much time studying.

This is precisely why Sally and so many of her advisor colleagues are not trusted by their clients. They enjoy the academic side of their work but not the client-facing aspect. Because they do not see themselves as business people, they will never have the enjoyment and profitability they deserve. They need to readjust their thinking.

Many years ago, I was an expert on Development Land Tax. On 10 July 1985, Nigel Lawson, the Chancellor of the Exchequer, abolished it. There was thereafter no need for advice on this tax. My expertise was suddenly worthless.

I looked around for other areas where clients may have need of advice. They were increasingly buying houses and businesses abroad, so I began looking into cross-border succession. I could see that anti-avoidance taxation was growing ever more complex and, as I was not enjoying it so much, I decided to move in a different direction.

You may be the world's leading expert on insolvency, but if no one is going insolvent that knowledge will have little value. Being in business is all about doing what your clients want, and if you are an advisor, that means advising your client in the areas where they need advice. For an expert to define themselves by their area of expertise and knowledge is to miss the point – it is valueless unless a client needs that advice and is prepared to pay for it.

Are your bills paid on time without complaint?

If your bills are not being paid on time and in full, you need to ask yourself why. Your clients should pay for your expertise in solving their problems in a timely fashion. If the clients do not recognize they have a problem or that your advice provides them with a resolution to that problem, they will not value your work and will resist paying you.

Put another way, do you care for your clients or are they only an afterthought to the work you are doing for them?

One firm I consulted for cherished their network of intermediaries, but did not have an up-to-date list of their clients. I was amazed. It's the clients who pay the bills, not the intermediaries! How can you start to keep in touch or trickle in some repeat business if you do not even know who your clients are?

Furthermore, the 'lock up' days in this organisation were averaging just over six months: clients were not paying bills for about half the year and when they did, they were more than likely to negotiate a discount. Why was this business subsidizing their clients' cash flow – was it a bank? If it was, it would charge interest, but this business was so frightened of losing its clients, it accepted the situation as normal.

When bills are not being paid in a prompt fashion, something is wrong and you need to find out what that problem is if you want to continue to draw a salary and earn a bonus. Late payment of bills indicates client dissatisfaction. And that is a signal that urgent attention is needed.

In a survey of ninety advisors on private client legal services, a staggering **100%** said they should keep their clients updated more regularly.

Most clients only find out what progress is being made when they receive a bill with an itemized breakdown – this is invariably a nasty shock – and results in a resistance to paying bills.

Three months after the survey came out, I asked the private client department of the law firm I was consulting whether they had taken any action in response to it. Not one advisor had implemented any changes in their reporting to clients and there was no improvement on lock up days.

Business is not a dirty word; it merely means doing what your clients want in a way that makes them feel you care, and for a price which is commensurate with the value they perceive.

Clients, not customers

The first step to gaining the trust of your clients is to put them at the center of the business. Not intermediaries, products or services – clients.

> The trustee's obligation is... to act in the best interests of the beneficiaries.

What is 'trust'? It is important to know because it gives some insights into what a 'trusted relationship' means. The legal entity called a 'trust' is not a contract, which is between two people; it is a three-way arrangement. The 'settlor' gives an asset or assets to someone as a 'trustee' to manage and deal with on 'trust', for the benefit of another, the beneficiary. The trustee's obligation is 'fiduciary' which means to act in the best interests of the beneficiaries. This means knowing them intimately and deciding what is best for them as people; for some it may mean giving a loan to start a business, but for other clients this may not be at all appropriate.

To build a 'trusted advisor' relationship with a client is to act in their best interests rather than your own. If a prospective client says, "I want to live in Switzerland to avoid paying capital gains tax on the sale of my business," you could simply go through all the details on how to become a resident of Switzerland, what he could do to become non-resident of the UK and then charge a big fat fee. But if you knew that he'd just had a grandson, you could point out that becoming non-UK resident would mean he may not be close enough to watch his grandson grow up. You could advise him to give some thought as to which was more important; watching his grandson grow up or saving tax. This is client care in action.

I have seen so many tax exiles sitting in their chosen country, with more money than they would have otherwise had, but miserable, missing their friends and family. For many, the move just was not worth it.

> Showing clients you care, even though you may begin by not earning a fee, will reap rewards further down the track.

How, I hear you ask, does caring for your client make money if you are turning work away all the time? In Chapter 4 I will explain in more detail how human beings love to be cared for and, if they believe that you are actually looking after their interests and not yours, they are many more times likely to give you repeat business and recommend you to a friend. Showing clients you care, even though you may to begin with not earning a fee, will reap rewards further down the track.

Know your clients

Do you have an up-to-date list of your clients, the bills they have paid, when they were paid and how much discount has been applied? Do you know what the work was for, who did it and where it came from?

Those who are late in paying their bills need to be contacted and asked why. In most cases, there will be some dissatisfaction with the service or lack of communication; only rarely will it relate to criticism of the actual work done. Hourly billing is particularly disliked.

Advisors do not like spending time explaining what they were doing for clients and reporting back. In particular they hate billing because it involves reporting progress and feedback to the client, and it isn't always good news. When the survey asked the ninety advisors why they reported so infrequently, they replied that they wanted to keep costs down to stop the clients complaining.

This is to miss the point entirely. Their clients were rich and could pay for their services. Clients were resisting fees due to a lack of client care, not because of poor quality of work. They don't just want the work to be done: they want to feel involved, and they want to be included in the decision making. Advisors need to understand that clients have problems concerning their money and they need to take decisions about it. These are decisions they have to make; they must not blindly follow what their advisors tell them. For them to make decisions, they need to be informed and kept in regular contact, not ignored until such time as a bill needs to be paid.

Advisors whose bills are always paid late need some training in client care and their progress needs to be monitored. If no improvement is made then they may be more suited to working for institutions, where client care is not so important.

If a job is making a loss, whether it's due to a lack of care from the advisor, or because a client is wasting their advisor's time, then it should be reviewed and, if necessary, terminated. Professional advisors are not in business to make a loss and clients need to understand this just as clearly as the advisors do.

How much wriggle room does your client have?

An advisor acting for UHNW individuals must accept that they can be as irrational as they please; it is their money and if they want to blow the lot on a horse running at 2.30 at Newbury, there is no one who can stop them. Clients do not always do what they are told and neither should they; advisors should continually remind themselves that the money is not theirs and their clients do not have to follow their advice, unless not doing so would be breaking the law.

Of course many parents do not want their children to squander their inheritance for fear that they will regret it later. Deciding on the right time for a child to inherit is never easy. Too soon and they may blow it, too late and they can become resentful.

Sasha was 19 when her father Stuart died. Stuart had been divorced from his wife Maria for a number of years and had gone on to remarry. Sasha's father was a very wealthy man with an extensive art collection and many millions. Under his will, Stuart left the majority of his estate to Sasha, and the house and a small allowance to Medina, his second wife. She had been expecting considerably more from her late husband. She'd nursed him devotedly in the last few years of his life

> Deciding on the right time for a child to inherit is never easy. Too soon and they may blow it, too late and they can become resentful.

and she begrudged Sasha's inheritance. She sued Stuart's executors, including David, Stuart's investment manager and trusted advisor, on the basis that she was a dependent of Stuart's and had not been properly provided for. The court was sympathetic and awarded her an increase, but it paled into insignificance beside Sasha's inheritance.

Sasha went to live in the South of France where she hosted lavish parties and was seen only in the best couture. David, who continued to manage Sasha's inheritance, despaired of her lavish expenditure and asked her to be less generous. He pointed out that the money would not last forever if she continued to spend at that rate, but Sasha saw him only as a killjoy; she was worth millions, she was a very wealthy woman. She refused to listen to David, who was powerless to stop her spending; all he could do was warn her of the consequences. Everyone loved Sasha, but she was also feckless and spoilt.

Sasha demanded more and more money, and David could not withhold it from her – it was hers outright. By the time she was thirty-five, the music stopped. David's warnings came true. Her money was running out and now she had to retrench. She bought a home in Oxfordshire and taught yoga and Pilates, which at least gave her an income. Eventually David told her that she had to sell the house and live abroad because she simply could not make ends meet.

Inheritance issues

Francis, on the other hand, was always told that he would inherit on the death of his mother, April. Under her husband's will, April was given a life interest in a trust, which meant that she was entitled to the income for her life from the investments in the trust. James and John were the trustees. April was only 63 when her husband died and Francis was 28. His mother was in good health so he had no option but to knuckle down.

Francis badgered James and John for an advance for his business, which after much nagging, they conceded to. For a while he did very well and had no further need for cash. Francis was lucky; he sold his business at the top of the market and went to live for a couple of years in Spain, playing golf and tennis. But Francis grew bored and invested his sale proceeds into a hotel complex that went horribly wrong. He lost £8 million and decided to return to the UK to work. By this time the recession was in full bloom and he struggled. Francis went back to James and John to ask for more money. He knew that if he continued to whinge and whine, they would eventually give him the money – much to the chagrin of his sister.

April was then diagnosed with cancer, and one could not help but notice a look of delight creep across Francis' face. But his mother was tough and she was not going to die to suit her son. Sadly the relationship between Francis and his mother during the last few months of her life was not happy; she felt he would prefer her dead and resented him for that. Ironically, Francis was making serious revenue from a new joint venture when his mother died. At the time of her death, he had little need for her money, but the damage had been done. He felt guilty and regretted his greed for his inheritance for many years thereafter.

Can wealth owners spend their money without restriction?

A family office may have a mission statement to guide them in making their decisions, but ultimately the family or founder can do with his or her money as they choose.

If however wealth is held in a trust, there is less wriggle room. The trustee must follow the terms of the trust and the law relating to trustees, which obliges them to act in the best interests of their clients. It is the trustees who decide what is in the best interests of the beneficiaries and not the beneficiaries themselves. The trustees do however need to account to the beneficiaries for the assets under their control, but do not need to give reasons for their decisions. It is the trustees' strict duty to look after the best interests of the beneficiaries; it is called a fiduciary duty of care.

Charles is a beneficiary of a trust under which he is entitled to the income. He will not get the capital until he is forty. When he was at university, he went through a wild phase, taking drugs and indulging in a night club business. The trustees decided to invest the monies in the trust in low income producing investments to increase the capital gain to which Charles was not

> It is the trustees' strict duty to look after the best interests of beneficiaries... Less strict is the obligation of a director to his shareholders.

entitled and reduce the income to which he was entitled. He demanded to see the investment portfolio of the trust and queried the spread of investments, pointing out that if they reinvested he could have a better return. The trustees refused to alter their investment policy until several years later when he was much more settled and reliable.

Less strict is the obligation of a director to his shareholders. Directors also have a duty to maximise the returns of the business for their shareholders, but it is not as strict as the fiduciary duty of a trustee. Furthermore, if the shareholders do not like what the directors are doing with their business, they can have them removed. Beneficiaries cannot remove a trustee unless between them they represent all the interested parties. If some of the beneficiaries are as yet unborn, trustees can only be removed if there is either a power in the trust deed or if the disgruntled beneficiaries go to court.

Knowing how much wriggle room a client has with regard to their wealth can make a big difference to the way an advisor should address his or her client. If a client has a lot of wriggle room, and can spend his or her money without restriction, there is no obligation on them to be rational. As an investment manager, you may want to preserve wealth, and as a succession lawyer, you may want to make sure it is passed on to the next generation; but if your clients want to spend it, or give it to charity, they can.

Your subconscious

Have you ever been at a party chatting to someone and then out of the blue heard your name? How did you hear it over all the noise? Have you ever heard a mother tell her child, "Don't run," and the child immediately starts running? Or you say to yourself, "Why am I so clumsy?" and immediately drop something?

Your subconscious or reticular activating system is continually working; trying to solve problems, and looking out for things of interest. But, like a child who is told 'not' to run and immediately starts running, it cannot process a negative.

This is why there are so many self-help books teaching how to develop a positive attitude, because each time you chide yourself, or get cross with yourself, you are perpetuating the wanting or worse, what you do not want.

Every time you ask yourself, "Why do I have so little money?" the subconscious hears "so little money" and looks for ways to perpetuate this. If you continually say, "Why is it always me who has to do all the hard work?" it hears "hard work" and looks for more opportunities to work hard.

This is why setting goals – or setting dreams – which is a nicer way of saying the same thing, is such a good thing. Furthermore, these goals need to be repeated time and again and measured for progress until they become ingrained in the subconscious.

> Your subconscious or reticular activating system is continually working; trying to solve problems, and looking out for things of interest.

It is also of fundamental importance to express your goals in the present, not the future. Say, "Today, I will have a good day," and the subconscious hears this as nothing to deal with right now. However, if it's phrased as, "Today is a good day," the subconscious is activated to make it a good day.

A very powerful way to set goals is to have a workshop and to do it collectively. Be careful that the session does not start by looking at the problems. Statements such as, "We do this every year and it's always the same; every year we fail," is not going to set the right tone – be positive, be pleased, live life as if you chose every detail.

Vision statement

When you, know where you are going, and you may like to use the training material at the end of this chapter to help you, you can start to write your vision statement. This should include not only what you want to do and with whom, but also your values and principles. This is important because your business needs a personality, which in marketing language is called its 'brand' or 'voice'. Get the best people in a room and brainstorm what that brand looks like.

I was fortunate enough to attend such a workshop. The people in the room were asked for adjectives to describe an Audi. Up came 'reliable', 'dependable', 'safe', and so on. Then they were asked to describe Apple; up came 'stylish', 'easy to use', 'great service', and 'innovative'. Then they were asked for adjectives to describe a private bank: 'expensive', 'arrogant', 'self- serving', 'aloof', 'complacent', and so on.

That is not a good brand image! But it would be a mistake to think that the brand is weak; it isn't. It is the personality that needs changing – and no spin exists that can change a personality disorder.

Transformation depends on everyone within the organisation changing their attitude. They all need to be facing in the right direction. Everyone has to embrace the tone and values of the business as it wants to be. To my mind, the best way of doing this is to start at the grass roots and work upwards and avoid any form of branding consultant until you have some idea as to what it is you want to achieve.

Do you remember when British Airways was rebranded with colourful tail pieces? Mrs Thatcher, then Prime Minister, was not amused. She expressed her disappointment by simply taking off her scarf and placing it over the model plane they were looking at. What was wrong with being proud to be British?

Of course, very soon thereafter the company reinstated the Union Jack.

Your vision statement must be written in the present tense in positive language. It must be agreed by all parties and referred to regularly. It must also be referred to whenever difficult decisions need to be made, such as who to recruit, who to let go and in what to invest. The vision statement needs to be central to the ongoing business, not just written and left in a drawer – paste it up in the coffee area, canteen and include it in your brochures and marketing literature.

Now we know where we are going, we need to plan how to get there.

If you would like to know more, about how to set goals simply scan the code, or copy this link **http://www.garnhamfos.com/wbfpc-extras/ chapter-1** for some training tips that will assist you.

Now you know where you want to go, you need to plan as to how you are going to get there, which we cover in the next chapter.

Chapter 2
Planning for advisors

Chapter summary:

- Caring for clients wins more business.

- The importance of gaining your clients' trust.

- SMART networks: create your A list.

- SMART networks: manage your network.

- SMART networks: use case studies to keep your contacts updated.

Most advisors love their expertise, not their clients

Why is it that some advisors are trusted and others are not? The secret is that those who are trusted care for their clients; they have a mindset of what can I give, not what can I get. It may seem illogical and even bad for business to care for clients, but we have to remember that we are human and we don't tend to behave rationally. It is because we like people who care for us and want to do business with them that a culture of care makes good commercial sense, but we need to know how it works as we plan for our success as a trusted advisor.

Caring and winning business are completely compatible, but it's not immediately obvious how this works.

Choose your clients carefully

If you are not making a profit on a client, do not lavish time and energy on them; they are simply not worth it. This is why you need to know what your best work is and who your best clients are. These are the clients on whom you want to exercise your care and attention.

This exercise should not be done lightly. You may *think* that some clients are profitable in some areas, but you need to know rather than guess. You are in business to advise and to make a profit. If you do not, you will not be paid, neither will you get a bonus and, in the worst case scenario, you will be out of a job.

So before you start putting your culture of care into practice, you need to know who you should be showering your affection on and who's just not worth the effort. Only follow up and make time for those clients who are worth it. If you have clients who are not making you a profit, then you need to adopt a different strategy.

George has twenty clients. He lists them according to fees earned, speed with which they pay his bills, work done for them and time spent. From this simple exercise, he can see which work and clients are making the most profit for him and focus his business on getting more clients and work like that.

Focus on your client, not your expertise

By acting in your clients' best interests, you are also more likely to provide a better service and win more business. If you look only after your own interests, you could lose out.

Shaun, a private client lawyer, specialises in immigration, succession and cross-border issues. Juan is an ideal client and Shaun wants to build a good relationship with him. To do so, he needs to focus his attention on the client rather than his expertise; he has to work out what he can do for Juan, not how much money he can make out of Juan in fees. If Shaun's mind is set on Juan and Juan's needs and wants, he is more likely to win his trust and form a long-lasting relationship.

Shaun knows he can assist Juan, but first he needs to find out what Juan's concerns are. At the first meeting, Juan explains that he has come to see Shaun because he wants to take advantage of the favourable tax advantages for non-UK domiciled residents in the UK. However, he says, he's just found out that his old school – where he'd planned to send his daughters – was full. Now he does not know what to do. Shaun gives Juan the name of a consultant who can introduce him to other schools. Juan is very grateful: he was worried about his daughters and Shaun helped him find a solution.

The fact that Juan attended this school puts Shaun on notice that his potential client already has a connection with the UK. He asks Juan why he was moving to the UK and why he had been to school there.

Shaun finds out that Juan was coming over to help his father build up their beef export business and to help his elderly mother who lives in the UK. Another alarm bell – his mother lives in the UK.

Juan tells Shaun about his mother. She'd gone to Argentina as a young woman and had met and fallen in love with a good looking polo player. When she became pregnant he refused to marry her, but agreed to take on the child and bring it up as his own in Argentina. His mother returned to England.

Juan had been to an English boarding school so he could be close to his mother, but he still maintained his roots in Argentina.

The fact that Juan was born to an unmarried English woman, had attended an English school, and was returning to live in the UK with his family changes everything.

If Shaun had simply run through the immigration rules and favourable tax rules for non-UK domiciled individuals, he would have missed some vital clues that would affect his advice. Juan had been to school in the UK, had an English mother, was born

> If Shaun had rushed in... He would probably have given wholly inappropriate advice and missed out on the bigger work.

illegitimately, and was now returning to England. These facts are likely to mean that Juan has a UK domicile; he is therefore not entitled to the favourable tax treatment available for non-UK domiciled people.

Shaun now needs to explain this to Juan and ask some more questions about his plans. He discovers that Juan is not wealthy himself, which means there is little advantage in him being non-UK domiciled. Both his mother and father are wealthy, however. His father wants him to take over the business and his mother wants him to inherit her wealth. Already the goal posts have shifted. What had turned out to be a small immigration and tax matter has turned into a full scale cross-border succession plan.

If Shaun had rushed into giving advice, he could very well have advised Juan on the basis that he was non-UK domiciled and a wealthy individual, when in fact he was neither. He would probably have given wholly inappropriate advice and missed out on the bigger work.

Your clients are not experts – go at their pace

When acting for a private client, try not to make assumptions. Maud wanted succession advice so her advisor, Grant, assuming he knew what she wanted, told her how much it would cost. She was horrified. Grant thought he knew what she needed to do and told her. He may even have believed that he was caring for her. He may have worked for people like her for years and has insights and experience as to the dangers, the pitfalls and the opportunities. Grant can probably see what she needs and, if she accepts his advice, would save time, money and problems down the line. But if Maud is not ready for Grant's advice and he has not yet won her trust, then resistance is inevitable.

Grant needs to take a deep breath, sweep aside his superior knowledge and take Maud from where she is to wherever she is capable of going. To begin with, this may be only a relatively small piece of work. Grant

> Pride has to be swallowed if an advisor genuinely intends to care for a client.

needs to phone the following month to ask how she's getting on. Maud would be delighted to hear from Grant and would no doubt want to see him about some other small matter. Then a month later, he can phone again... And so on.

Although it may take Grant several years to get Maud to where he could have taken her in a few months, had she accepted his advice in the beginning, and for considerably less in fees, Maud is happy because Grant took her at her pace, not his.

Pride has to be swallowed if an advisor genuinely intends to care for a client. Firstly, you have the knowledge and expertise to assist them, secondly, you have your own agenda, with goals and targets to meet, and thirdly, there is an underlying irritation that if only the client would listen, you could fix what they wanted quickly, efficiently and effectively.

It is tempting to think how much easier it would be if clients just stepped aside and let you get on with it. But this attitude does not fit with caring for your client. If they are not ready for your super-charged professionalism, you have got to win their trust first before *gently* guiding them to where your knowledge and expertise can take them.

The reason why so many advisors are not trusted is because they get frustrated with their clients. Of course, they don't know everything the advisor knows! Don't treat them like idiots – they're not. The advisor must learn to take their client with them. If the matter is complicated, learn how to explain the concepts in a way they can understand.

It helped me to think of my clients as children of different ages. Children are not stupid, neither are they slow; they are simply not fully mature. If you took your four-year-old skiing, you would be patient, choose your route carefully, make sure you avoided the ice sections and give them regular encouragement. If, on the other

> The advisor must learn to take their client with them. If the matter is complicated, learn how to explain the concepts in a way they can understand.

hand, you took your thirteen-year-old skiing, it would be a completely different scenario; you would probably have to ski as fast as you could to keep up.

You may think I am being disrespectful in thinking of some of the richest people in the world as children, but they have become rich by knowing everything they need to know in running their own business. They have not spent the last twenty years in your area of expertise, and often have no idea just how complex and disharmonious laws and investments can be. As an advisor, you are there to advise. They do not need to know all you know, they are coming to you for advice, and they need to know what the problems are and how to fix them.

Choose clients you like

There is another reason why you need to choose your clients carefully. Some teachers are good at teaching children of nursery age, others a little older and some are professors at university. Personally, I liked working for high- end entrepreneurs, people who had a background in business. These people fascinated me – they were focused, ruthless, and most had in some way or another suffered, regrouped and carried on. I had endless patience with them because I felt so honoured to work with them. I knew that to work for them I had to earn their trust, and some clients would take longer to give their trust than others.

Other advisors like to work for clients who are more vulnerable, like the elderly, widows and orphans. Others like to work with clients who have similar interests, whether art, shooting, football, cricket or fishing. If you share similar interests to your clients, you are far more likely to be tolerant and go at their pace, not yours.

Why some advisors are poor at caring for clients

You arrive at your new office as an advisor and are told that the first two weeks will be devoted to training. You are taught the firm's processes, what forms need to be filled in, and the compliance issues.

Then you are trained on the firm's products (possibly the most profitable ones), the computers, and learn all about time entries and billing. You are told about the firm, the different departments, human resources, training opportunities, ongoing CPD points, recruitment and ongoing assessment, probably a bit about its history, and regulatory issues. Lastly, you are told what the firm expects of you, your targets, and bonus expectations.

Some organisations are ruthless; they have identified what makes them the most money and expect their sales teams to make a target number of phone calls every day to sell them. That may be good for business but it is not enjoyable, and has resulted in FCA fines for mis-selling. Clients don't like it much either. If you don't want to work for

> You need to think SMART, not HARD.

such an organisation, then don't – there are others who realise that a consultative type of selling is more profitable in the long term, even though the sale takes time to build.

You go back to your desk and hear Jamie at the next station arranging to have coffee. Who is he having coffee with? He tells you that he likes to keep up with his network. He also tells you proudly that he has 1,224 people with whom he is connected on LinkedIn. Jamie is considered really successful in the office so you decide to follow his lead. This is 'learning on the job' or, put another way, 'picking up other people's bad habits'.

You need to stop right there: think SMART, not HARD. You have analysed the clients you want, what your best work is, and what you want to do for them. You also know what sort of client you like working with, a high-end entrepreneur, or someone who likes shooting or fishing. Where are you likely to find them?

How do advisors win new business and why?

In business, what you need to do is find what works and do more of it; it is as simple as that. So let's look at how the wealth advisory industry wins new business and then think SMART.

Traditionally, there are only two routes to market to win new business: making more out of what you've got (which I will deal with in Chapter 7), and networking.

All UHNW individuals need an advisor to help them manage their wealth. All UHNWs will need to put in a tax return and must have a bank for the safe custody of their wealth. By definition, all UHNW individuals in the world can be contacted once removed through their advisors.

> ...there are only two routes to market to win new business: making more out of what you've got and networking.

Furthermore, if the advisor wants to build a trusted relationship with his or her clients, they use their extensive knowledge about them to find ways to assist. As we have already seen, this means recommending the services of those in their network to their clients. A referral of business to a key member in your network in this manner means they get a qualified lead, pre-screened by you network and you are on the way to building a trusted relationship with your client.

Liz is an estate agent. She knows that Juan is coming from Argentina and she has been looking to buy a house for him and his family. She already knows a lot of valuable information about him, which she can use to help Juan and build trust, but also to strengthen the ties with her network. She's worked with Juan for several months and has got to know him quite well. If she focuses merely on her expertise, she will be missing out on a valuable opportunity to use the information she has gleaned about Juan to win her new business.

As it begins to look as if a purchase is going to proceed, she will ask Juan who he'll use to do the legal work for his purchase. If he doesn't have a lawyer, this is her first opportunity to make a recommendation. But she should not stop there. She may have been sent a case study written by Shaun about the work he did for a client who came to the UK to live with his family and for whom he did some tax planning as a non-

UK domiciled person before he became a resident. Juan is delighted with Liz because it shows that she cares for him. She has introduced him to someone who could sort out his tax arrangements. In this way she is building trust with Juan, which she should use to her advantage.

A month after the sale, Liz phones Juan to find out how he is getting on. He tells her that Shaun did a great job for him, introduced him to Jason who helped him with schools for his daughters, and is now working on a succession plan. He also tells her that he's bought some new art which looks stunning in the flat and is starting a collection.

This is another opportunity for Liz. She asks him where he bought the art and whether he has proper insurance for it. She can now recommend Juan to an insurance broker and of course let the insurance broker know that she has done so.

It's not about quantity, it's about quality

Jamie may have 1,224 followers on LinkedIn, but what do they do and how can they help him? Jamie doesn't know. If you are serious about winning new business and networking efficiently, you need to adopt a culture of care and do some more homework. What are the services or products your clients need?

She needs to be ruthless about her contact lists. If a contact, has neither the clients she is looking for or has services her clients could use, or are not the professionals she would like to refer business they need to be axed: they will not refer work to her and she will not be referring work to them. At this point, Liz may also realise that although she knows most people in her network well, she probably does not know what they do. She must now begin to find out.

We show how easy this is to do in our Books Extra Training Material which you can access at the end of this chapter.

Don't be afraid to care

I often hear advisors saying they are the last in the food chain or don't get the opportunity to refer clients. This is the answer you'll get from any advisor who has not really thought about their clients – what they may want and how they can help them to build a trusted relationship. These advisors tend only to talk about their work with the client and don't think of the wider picture of the client's needs and requirements. If the advisor genuinely cared for their clients, they would be actively seeking ways in which they could assist. It is through taking an active interest in their client that the advisor will build trust, get repeat business, and referral work from their network.

The most valuable resource any advisor to the UHNW community has is their client base and, by caring for them, they can win more business. A note of warning: successful advisors only care for those who are worth it. This way, they steer clear of unprofitable work.

Actively manage your network

If you have a good spread across a wide range of disciplines, it is absolutely vital at this stage to manage your network. In most organisations, there will be some form of client relationship management system. You will need to run such a system for your network. You need to record what work your network does, how often you have referred business to them, how many times you have gone out with them for a coffee or tea, and how often they have shared your case studies and testimonials with their clients.

Having an active network should be a two-way street. It is simply not true of any advisor that they are the last in the food chain and have no reciprocation work to give.

The reason why advisors do not reciprocate business is either because they do not care for their clients or do not know what you do well enough to recommend you. You need to make sure your network has the information it needs to be able to make recommendations. As we will see in part four, the easiest way to assimilate new concepts is through case studies, so make the most of them.

Keep up with your network

Now that you know who is on your network A list and what services they provide, you need to initiate regular meaningful dialogue. One strategy that works well is to invite your network to regular meetings. You could suggest that your A list advisors meet at your office for an update on what they've been doing with their clients for the past month. Case studies are a good way to do this.

Then you can have few drinks afterwards. I will go into this means of 'active networking' later in the book.

As you prepare your case studies for this meeting, you can compile them into a useful newsletter about the work you do for your clients. You can leave this in your reception, on your website, and refer to it on LinkedIn. Your newsletter could be regularly sent out to your network B list.

If you're not confident about your writing, or are concerned that it would identify your clients, hire a copywriter or journalist to do it for you. You simply need to tell them what you've been doing for which clients and let them write it up for you.

> Make sure that you regularly prune and tend your list of advisors.

Make sure that you regularly prune and tend your lists of advisors. You may need to move some from your B list to your A list and vice versa as you see who networks well and who not.

UHNWs often stay with the same advisors even though they are dissatisfied with them because they simply do not know where to find anyone who can serve them better. Advisors who care for their clients should be able to help them find new advisors who are much more in tune with their needs.

In many cases, referrals tend only to be made when the client asks for a recommendation. This should not be the norm if an advisor genuinely cares for his or her client and knows what problems are being solved by those in his or her network. If an advisor is truly operating from a culture of care, referrals will be made on a daily basis.

If you would like to know more about how to plan simply scan the code below or copy the link **http://www.garnhamfos.com/wbfpc-extras/ chapter-2-training-material** for training tips which will assist you.

Now you know how to plan, you need to manage you time, which we cover in the next chapter.

Chapter 3
Time management for advisors

Chapter summary:

- Are you busy – or productive?

- Make a list and manage your time.

- Is travel really necessary?

- The benefits of online networking.

- 'Busy fools' put their lives and well-being on the line.

Time unites everyone, but do we use it wisely?

Wasting time is, to my mind, a sin. I am not talking about spending time pleasurably or taking time to reflect or meditate – these pursuits are not a waste of time. Time is very much like wealth; once it is gone, it is gone. You cannot get it back. Just as some people squander money, many of us are guilty of squandering time.

If we are serious about making and smashing our goals, we need to be serious about not wasting time. All humans are the same, whether UHNW individuals or advisors, so in this section I haven't made any distinction between the two communities.

I want to go through my eight steps of how time is thrown away to enable us to focus on making the best use of it so we can attain and exceed our goals.

Proactive, not reactive: do you have a minute?

I have had the honour of working with some hugely successful individuals who are, almost without exception, generous with their time – because they are proactive and not reactive.

Is this you?

You get to your desk to find 40 unopened emails and two letters. You start on the emails and the first requires you to open a folder and refresh yourself on some details, but you haven't got time for that.

> Lack of time management is not only detrimental to your health; it is also stopping you from achieving your goals.

You move on to the next, the phone rings, a colleague wants to drop in for a chat, he is concerned about a sensitive issue, you look at the calendar and make a time to meet. You go back to your emails and delete a few, then your assistant comes in.

"Do you have a minute?" You like to keep an open door policy, so you chat to your assistant until the telephone rings; your assistant waits while you take the call, and then your secretary comes in with some magazines and post, you glance through the magazines and a press release about a client catches your eye, you add it to the pile on your desk that you fully intend to read later.

If this sounds familiar, you are working in a reactive and not a proactive manner, your business is running you – and you are not running your business.

You are allowing people to interrupt your life with, "Do you have a minute?" meetings, telephone calls and emails that disturb you all day long, leaving you with only your free time to plan and do what you need to do to make and smash your goals. This lack of time management is not only detrimental to your health and home life; it is also stopping you from achieving your goals.

Time managers and time wasters

I was always amazed at how calm my UHNW clients were when I was a leading private client lawyer. I came to the conclusion that these captains of industry were more disciplined and organised with their time than most advisors.

Firstly, if someone said, "Have you got a minute?" the answer would be, "No. Book a time in the diary and come prepared with an agenda, considered questions and a suggestion about the solution." In this way, both sides were prepared to consider the issue, quietly and without interruptions, and the result was usually much more worthwhile.

The second great interrupter is the telephone. If you don't have a secretary and you've allocated time to a meeting or working on a project, set a voicemail that says you're working and will call back later, with a request to know what the call was concerning. Nine times out of ten, a call is not worth taking, because it could either have been dealt with by someone else, or the matter has passed.

Emails are a third source of distraction and interruption. Once again, it's not necessary to deal with these immediately; do what you've planned to do and then make time to work through all of them. Some of you may laugh – I have a poor reputation for answering emails, because for a long time I did not allocate time to dealing with them. The same principle applies to LinkedIn, Twitter, Instagram and other social media platforms.

One word of warning to the 'I am so busy' junkie. If you start becoming proactive and stop being reactive, it will feel like you are not very busy. This is not a comfortable feeling for those who measure their

> It's not about how busy you are – it's about how productive you are.

importance by how much they are in demand. Once again, it comes down to what you are trying to achieve; are you trying to make and smash your goals? Then you need to free up more time to do so.

Are you fooling yourself into thinking that 'no-one could be working harder at making their goals happen'? It's not about how busy you are – it's about how productive you are. If you're being productive, you really need to be more disciplined and focused on running your business rather than letting it run you.

Touch it once and list making

I am fortunate to be a Trustee of the Household Cavalry Museum which is in the corner of the Parade Ground just off St James's Park, backing onto Whitehall. The Household Cavalry are the soldiers on the black horses that guard the official entrance to Buckingham Palace off Whitehall and have those amazing fountain-like plumes cascading from their helmets.

One of the time management lessons taught in the army is to touch something only once; decide there and then what you are going to do with what you have touched, and when. Put it on your list and in your diary. With regard to emails, make some files called Prepare, Action, Reading and Waiting. When you read them, make sure you filter according to author or subject so that you deal with all aspects relating to that project together. This saves a huge amount of time and ensures you don't miss important relevant messages.

Be absolutely insistent that everyone puts the same subject heading in the subject line, so important messages don't slip or get overlooked. Also insist that emails cover one issue only so that they can be read with others on that issue and can be filed appropriately as well. Ban emails that deal with a range of issues; they will waste your time and could lead to important information slipping through the net. If you can't leave an email unanswered, turn off the alert button. Make sure you are in control of your emails: do not let them control you.

Make sure that every time you touch something and cannot deal with it there and then that it is filed in a pending file, **and** included in a list.

Now you need to manage your list. You need to make an A list and a B list. Ask yourself, "What are the eight most important things to do today that will help me achieve my goals?" This is your A list. You should never have more than eight things on your A list because it will overwhelm you and the big, important things that need to be done to make and smash your goals simply won't get done.

As you cross things off your A list, you will need to add to it from your B list. Personally, I prefer not to revise my lists as I cross each one off. It is psychologically good to see the list diminish during the day. I prune and rearrange the lists on a daily basis according to priorities, but it is these lists that keep my time management under control.

> What are the eight most important things I need to do today that will help me achieve my goals?

I also include in these lists a number of personal items, which otherwise I would just not get done, in my enthusiasm to tick items off my list.

1. List management: prioritise and plan

As you prepare your lists, allocate time and a priority level to them. Let's say an invoice query comes in. You decide it will take half an hour, but it needs to be done urgently because it is important to you to manage clients and their expectations. You put this task into your A list and a less pressing matter you move down to your B list to do when you have a little more time.

Another trick is to do the hardest things that take the longest time in the morning and save the more pleasurable or shorter things for the afternoon, when you are feeling a little more tired.

I was involved in litigation which went on for several years – the email threads were incredible. Everyone was copied in to everything and felt it their duty to say something about everything. And so the bills kept going out and nothing got done. I was involved in another litigation that also went on for many years, but in this case the project was planned – who would receive what and report to whom. Although considerable time was spent in planning the project, years and millions of pounds

> Time management should be one of the crucial questions asked of an advisor who is billing on time...

were saved by planning how to handle things right at the start. You may say that planning saw the lawyers lose years of fees. That's true, but having seen the time wasted on the first project, I would emphatically not recommend that firm to another client or use them myself, while I certainly would with the second. Time management should be one of the crucial questions asked of an advisor who is billing on time, but from my experience no one ever asked me that question.

While on the subject of litigation, I have always taken the view that it should be the last resort because it is costly and time consuming. I've always favoured mediation. However, in light of recent experience, I would now say that it depends. If either side is totally intransigent or there is unlikely to be any movement, which is often the case with family disputes, sometimes going to court where a judge can make an order that is enforceable is the best and most cost-effective route. The earlier you take that route, the better so as not to allow entrenched positions to develop.

If a project is likely to take a long time, such as a report, drafting a contract or reading a detailed letter, you need to break it down into manageable chunks and allocate time over a period to get it done. I love large projects, but there are many people who put them off because they see it as a massive task. It is like the children's joke: "How do you eat an elephant? One bite at a time."

As you look at your A list, put 'to do' tasks in your diary and stick to those times and dates. It chunks up your day and makes you feel in control. It also stops any temptation to allow the "Do you have a minute?" meetings to creep back because your diary clearly tells you that you do not. You have allocated your time to something that needs doing now, so book a time when the 'just a minute' query can be dealt with according to priority. Make sure you allocate the requisite amount of time needed to deal with it.

If you are running a business, you need to make sure that not only you, but all your team are making lists, prioritising and planning their day. A small but focused team always outperforms larger and disorganised teams.

2. List management: short communications and clean desks

If you are making lists and prioritising your day, you should not have anything on your desk and all your communications should be brief.

I found a clean desk policy one of the hardest things to implement. Having a busy desk made me feel busy, but in fact most of what was on my desk was clutter that I never looked at. Furthermore, when I did make an attempt to tame my feral desk, I was often surprised by what was on it. When I tried to find something, it always took a long time, whereas if I had filed it when I had it in my hand, or thrown it away knowing that I had an electronic version in a file on my server, I'd have saved myself a lot of time and headaches.

> If you are making lists and prioritising your day, you should not have anything on your desk...

An extremely successful client of mine would physically tear up old drafts if they had been superseded. If you are doing things electronically, then you must make sure you date the draft and number it, so you always know which one is current.

It is well understood that 80% of filed information is never looked at again. So ask yourself, "If I need this in future, could I find it again from some other source?" I do a lot of writing and some ideas and articles trigger thoughts, so I put these into my reading file, and most things I store electronically and do not print out at all. As my desk became clearer, the better I got at managing my electronic filing system. I learned to file as I went along, but only if I needed the document later.

My UHNW community tends to write short messages such as, "Yes". If you top and tail every email with pleasantries, think of how many hours you must be wasting. Don't get me wrong, pleasantries are necessary for your best clients and the key people who help you achieve your goals, but they are just not needed for everyone all the time.

The other thing to watch is the time you take for a meeting. I used to work at Simmons & Simmons with Edward Troup, who subsequently became very senior in HM Treasury. He queried why meetings needed to last a whole hour. Most meetings can be over and done in much less time – but somehow they drag and drivel on until the full hour is up.

Provided it is made clear that the meeting will be short ("I think we can get through all we need within twenty minutes") and you have circulated this note before the meeting, then no one will be offended.

3. List management: do you have time for a coffee?

As a lawyer, before I adopted a very disciplined approach to winning business, I was astonished at how much time could be spent in having coffee. If each meeting lasted an hour, it can take hours and hours out of your day. When I first worked as a lawyer, it seemed that everyone was making time for coffee with anyone who suggested it. It seemed that this was what advisors did to win new business, but I couldn't understand why. When I took over as head of the group at Simmons & Simmons, I simply did not have the time for everyone who wanted to have coffee if I wanted to run the group and look after my clients. I needed to set goals and meet only those people who could be useful in getting me where I needed to go, otherwise it was a waste of time.

> Provided it is made clear that the meeting will be short... no one will be offended.

Once you have set your goals and you know who you want to target, may I suggest that you go back over your diary for the previous year and add up the time spent in meetings with people who are no longer on your list? How much time did you waste? Did these people ever refer any work to you?

Then it's a good idea to go over what you do before and after a meeting. How many meetings do you go to where you put the meeting in your diary but do not do any research on the person you are going to meet beforehand? Is there anything about them on LinkedIn? What does Google have on them? Is there anything on BConnect Club? Do they have a Twitter page? What is said about them on their website and in their brochure? After you've done your homework, you need to know what it is you want to achieve in some detail and make sure it is aligned to your goals – if not, the meeting will be a waste of time.

One of my most high profile clients had appointed a prominent gatekeeper to assist her in sorting out a few personal issues in a discreet and private manner. He invited me for a coffee. I knew that if we got on personally, I would remain appointed but if we didn't, I could lose the mandate.

It soon became obvious from my research that Michael, my client's gatekeeper, was keen on country sports, so one of my goals for the meeting was to steer the conversation to country sports, which was one of my hobbies at the time. It was very easy to engage him on his favourite pastime and it was easy thereafter to turn the subject to what he needed to do to assist his client. I easily won the business.

On another occasion, I had been doing some very low grade work for Roger, a whopper of a client, who I had not met in person. First I got to know his right-hand man and discussed some concerns before making a few suggestions as to how they could be resolved.

Roger was coming to London and, through his right-hand man, he agreed to have a coffee. I was warned that I'd probably get about ten minutes, if that, and had to get my message across effectively because I wouldn't have a second chance. I didn't have an opportunity to speak at the meeting because some other advisors were there too. As the ten minutes drew to a close, Roger turned to me and asked for my opinion on the issues. I had less than ten seconds. I had prepared what I was going say so delivered it in less than ten seconds. He smiled and told me I had the business.

On another occasion, I had a two hour preliminary meeting with advisors. After the meeting, Don, one of the advisors, telephoned us and said that our client, who was a very distinguished woman, was coming to London and wanted to meet for a coffee. He confided that she had a keen eye for fashion and would expect us to have the right type of handbags.

I went to the partnership to ask them for a 'firm's bag budget' which was based on the money we would have had to spend on flying to meet her, hotel accommodation and time out of the office. We arrived at the meeting and the three ladies in the team plonked their new handbags on the table. We won the business.

4. List management: travel – is it essential?

Travelling is such a waste of time. You need to ask yourself the question – why? Of course, you must travel to see clients, not all of them want or can come to see you. Most of the time, the clients will pay for your expenses, but not always for your time. When you factor in the time; travelling to the airport, waiting for the plane to take off,

> The focus is: think smarter; not harder.

flying, landing and getting to where you need to go, let alone the time when you are there, catching up on sleep, meetings and eating – is it worth it?

If it will help you achieve your goals, then every moment is time well-spent, but what about business development trips? I have seen colleagues spend hours and hours travelling abroad to see a list of contacts that have neither been qualified nor pre-screened. As a result, they get a lot of small ticket work and instructions from intermediaries, without working for the client direct.

The focus is: think smarter, not harder.

About fifteen or so years ago, we wanted to develop business relations in Switzerland, so we hired a decent venue and invited those we wanted to see to a small, intimate event. We made sure that we had done our homework on every single one of the attendees, especially on what would interest them.

Then we needed to make sure that what we did was clearly communicated to our chosen audience.

My preference was to give a talk liberally peppered with case studies so that what I did was clearly conveyed in the message. Everyone loves stories – and it is the easiest and most effective way to convey a message. Other advisors used role playing which was also very effective.

However, is there now any need to travel? Would it not be just as effective to arrange for the seminar or role play to be videoed and invite your audience to view it online? You can follow up by asking them whether your expertise is of any relevance to their clients, if they come back by saying yes – **then** follow up with a visit, if appropriate. When you meet them, you can reciprocate by asking what they do that could be of interest to your clients – in this way, you are building the basis of a reciprocal trusted relationship.

There are other things you can do remotely. If one of your key contacts resides abroad, you do not have to meet them to keep in touch. In fact, your connections could be more meaningful if you don't just rely on face-to-face contact. Let's say that you think Charlie has the sort of clients you'd also like as clients and is in a position to refer them to you for the work you are good at.

If you do your homework, you may discover that he's speaking at a conference in Miami. Rather than go to Miami, you could write to Charlie to say you've noticed that he's speaking, you're sorry you won't be there, but could he possibly send you his notes? If he does, read them and make comments. Make a point of saying that you have clients for which the work he does may be of interest. If he responds, you can tell him what you are doing for those clients and ask whether he has clients for which your services may be of use. If he doesn't have any such clients, move on; Charlie is a waste of time. However, if he says that his clients do need the services you provide from time to time, give him your full culture of care treatment. Follow what he does and make a point of continuing the dialogue, add him to your Google alerts, comment on his posts and the people with whom he is connected in LinkedIn; you have saved time and expense by not travelling and are on the way to winning new business, all from the comfort of your own office.

5. List management: networking

Everyone needs to network to win new business; some do it well and others do not. Let's take a typical networking scenario, such as a seminar or conference. You spend the time listening to speeches and then over coffee, lunch or tea, make as many connections and collect as many cards as you can.

> You need to pick the seminars or events that will put you in touch with people who are going to help you meet your goals.

You follow up or not, as the case may be.

From your goal setting, you will know what clients you're looking for and for what type of work. You need to pick the seminars or events that will put you in touch with people who are going to help you meet your goals.

Maybe you need to keep up to date, to learn or gain CPD points. This must be viewed separately from networking. At these types of seminars, you are likely to meet people like you with whom you may have interesting conversations, but you are unlikely to win new business because you are among your competitors.

Attending seminars to gain CPD points may no longer be the most cost-effective or time efficient way of learning. A far easier way to learn is online through videos, training modules and webinars.

Networking should be very focused; if the people you are meeting at an event are not in a position to assist you in winning your goals, don't go – what is the point? Of course, if you enjoy meeting people who won't assist you in getting to your goals, then recognise it for what it is – a social occasion. Don't kid yourself that in some fashion, it will win you new business. If the people you are meeting do not have the sort of clients you are looking for and cannot refer you the type of work you want, no matter how well you get on, you will simply not get any referral business.

The same is true of any other form of networking, such as Twitter, Facebook or LinkedIn. If you are connected to people who are not in a position to help you meet your goals, then what is the point in being connected and spending time connecting? Of course, it gives a nice warm feeling to know you have thousands of followers, but they need to be the right type and you only know this if you are certain of your goals and what you want to achieve.

> Online networking is far more effective and efficient than offline networking.

Network online as well, which is far more effective and efficient than offline networking. Follow those you think have clients that could be your ideal clients. Make sure they can see you and you can see them. Keep in touch and show an interest; it is far more effective than being in the same room and collecting a card.

Your time is precious

All work and no play is not a good balance. It is absolutely essential to factor in some 'you' time. If you are disciplined and focused and use the tips and tactics outlined above, you will have plenty of time not only for you, but also for your key clients when you are not charging them. You need to work out how best to use this time and this can be just as much a challenge as learning how to meet and smash your targets, whether it be with your wealth or working for people with wealth.

Many of the UHNW individuals I have worked with who are very focused on time management are also very clued up as to how to spend their spare time. Pierre would go fishing and I don't mean trout fishing, I mean deep sea fishing. He was brought up on and by the sea, so it was not a passion that he developed in his later years, it had been a passion since childhood. Of course, the fishing boat, which had a fighting chair in the middle surrounded by twelve rods and was managed by a gillie, was not large enough for him and his family and friends to sleep and relax, so he would moor it alongside his yacht, where he ate and slept. I was standing next to him on the yacht when his fishing boat came in sight. "Look at that, Caroline," he said. "What a beauty."

Another very wealthy man, Adrian, was not so keen on fishing as Pierrre, but liked his sailing. He also liked his comforts and his sleek sailing boat, for which he needed a crew of 12, was just too small to sleep and dine comfortably so he had what he called his 'kitchen' boat. This ocean-going yacht would go on ahead to a chosen destination so that by the time he and his crew had raced there, they could relax on the 'kitchen' boat and have a good meal without having to wait or go ashore. In both cases, and I could cite many more, the attention to detail and the planning was impressive.

For some, it has taken time to find out how they want to spend their spare time. As I said previously, the first five years following a liquidity event are the most vulnerable, and when coupled with the 'mortgages to management' anxiety, can be dangerous. It is often overlooked how many celebrities turn to drugs or drink to deal with this anxiety during this time; they are literally 'killing' time, but if not careful could also succeed in killing themselves.

This is when they need loved ones to understand what it is they are going through, or coaching and assistance so they can find their feet and a platform for their money.

Many advisors I have worked with have an unhealthy work/life balance. Male advisors have a tendency towards being busy fools, answering all the emails as they come in, and leaving meetings and mealtimes to answer calls. It was particularly prevalent in the company commercial departments when I started out my legal profession.

You would get a roomful of anything up to 20 advisors working to close a deal, all with their jackets off and many wearing braces. At about 10 p.m. they would send out for some food such as pizzas, which they'd eat, usually standing up. Hours would be wasted

> Are you are a 'busy fool' who has let work take control of your life? Then you are at risk.

as they waited for the documents to be amended and points finalised. They were all very earnest and serious, but a lot of it was a waste of time. The following day, they would be eager to tell their colleagues in hushed tones that it was 'an all-nighter'. Very often they would abandon dinner parties, theatre tickets and holidays to engage in sessions with the increasing risk of health problems, little time spent with the children and possibly even divorce.

There are a lot of self-help books on how to get back in touch with life, so I only want to make a few personal observations here. Are you a 'busy fool' who has let work control your life? Then you are at risk. If for whatever reason work stops, whether on retirement, or redundancy, a take-over, or a downturn in the market, you are in danger. If you don't have strong family bonds. you won't have support when you need it and you are likely to feel useless and a failure.

Simon was an extremely successful advisor who decided to take early retirement to focus for a year on a book he was writing. He confided in me after three months, saying that he felt a failure and a lack of respect. This was a man who was often called 'brilliant' by his peers. I assured him he was not a failure,

> 'Oblivion drinking' is on the increase among women advisors – especially amongst those who are juggling a family as well as a career.

it just felt like that because he wasn't as busy or in demand. It wasn't long before his book was finished, his brilliance more widely recognised and he was back in demand – possibly more so than before.

There is one danger that is on the increase for many women advisors – especially amongst those women juggling a family as well as a career – the tendency towards 'oblivion drinking'.

As they come home from a stressful day, and before they bathe the kids and prepare a meal for the family, they have a glass of wine, "to help me wind down". And after the family chores and evening meal, another glass or two follows to "help me sleep". The wine does not really aid sleep as it interferes with rapid eye movement, which is the deep cycle of sleep that aids memory and restores the body, and so the next day the body's ability to function is impaired. Weight is not lost, complexions are dulled and the woman feels more and more anxious – which leads to a further need for a drink.

There are personality types of women prone to this type of behaviour: the Pleasers, the Perfectionist, the Inner Critic and the Inner Child. I have come across many advisors who like to please their clients who are the last to leave the bar at conferences, pleasing everyone but themselves.

One of the most balancing and rewarding things I do is meditating every morning for half an hour. If normal life is like a child's snow dome, with the snow blurring the scene, then meditating is what happens when you stop shaking the dome. The snow starts to settle and things become clearer. I also walk in the park every day and this walk brings clarity and joy, which makes me feel good for the rest of the day. I have no idea whether my meditation is correct. I went to Asia to find out, but my guide said it was better not to interfere; it was working for me so he let me get on with it.

I also do some yoga, not for any other reason than I am getting older and need to remain supple. I also swim and like to cook and eat, but on the whole I prefer a life full of simple pleasures.

If you would like to know more, about how to manage time simply scan the code or copy the link **http://www.garnhamfos.com/wbfpc-extras/ chapter-3-training-material** for some marketing material which will assist you.

Now you know how to manage your time, you need to know how to get there, which we cover in the next chapter.

Chapter 4
Getting there for advisors

Chapter summary:

- Winning business: old money versus new money.

- Overcome prospects' fear of the influence of strangers

- Gain the power to influence.

- The value of intelligent giving.

- Case studies: attention, trust and business winners.

- Benefits of a digital platform.

Winning business from clients who want to remain private

UHNW individuals are by definition wealthy. Their wealth attracts all manner of people who want their wealth, whether for their philanthropic project, investment opportunities, or their products. To avoid this unwanted attention, they prefer to be private, mixing only with people like themselves and keeping away from anyone selling them anything.

They tend to dress inconspicuously, some taking it to extraordinary levels. After one pheasant shoot, I was invited to dinner and seated next to a gentleman who looked rather ragged. I wasn't sure whether he was the local tramp or the squire, so I had to tread carefully and ask lots of open questions. One clue was that he referred to his wife as her Ladyship and another was when he spoke of his children inheriting the estate. I finally worked out that he was a very distinguished Duke, but by his frayed jacket and scruffy hair, you would be more tempted to give him a fiver than refer to him as his Lordship.

When I was practicing law in Simmons & Simmons, I'd often say to my assistants, "Spot the professionals – they're always the better dressed." I remember going with one to see a client. My assistant was neatly suited and booted. When we left the meeting, he said, "Did you see? He had holes in his jacket and a button was missing from his shirt cuff." "Not unusual," I replied.

The other end of the spectrum also needs watching. Charlene is a very elegant and intelligent woman. She was getting a divorce from her husband of many years. She confided to me how her barrister made her feel ashamed of her lifestyle. "He seems to disapprove of my private plane, yacht, and island. I couldn't be sure he had my best interests at heart." He should not have made her feel ashamed; she was paying him. She decided in future to switch barristers. She did not want to engage someone who was critical or envious of her lifestyle – she was doing nothing wrong, just living her life the way she wanted.

This desire not to attract attention and to mix only with people who are as wealthy and with similar lifestyles can make UHNW individuals lonely. I was once fortunate to join Mark and his family on their private yacht. I was picked up by a chauffeur driven car, ferried to a private plane, then driven by another chauffeur driven car to a yacht to have dinner on board. It was wonderful not to have to queue to get onto the plane, not to have sleep cheek by jowl with strangers while flying, not to have to go through customs or wait for luggage coming off a conveyor belt – but I could see how travelling like that as a way of life could be lonely and isolating. Mark also worried when his daughter Melissa went clubbing and made sure she was accompanied by a security guard who kept a discreet distance but would whisk her away at the first sign of any trouble. Melissa and her father would have screeching rows about the level of security which he insisted upon, until one day one of her friends got kidnapped.

Winning business from such people is not easy, not only because they wish to remain private and do not want to mix socially with you, but also because they surround themselves with their inner sanctum and personal assistants. Any manner in which you try to contact them, whether by phone, email, post or pigeon, is likely to be intercepted and screened and will simply fail to be delivered. So how do you win new business from UHNW clients?

Your two most valuable assets in winning new business are your book of clients and your network. Clients want good service and your network wants new business. By adopting a culture of care to both communities, you can win new business. We will come onto providing your clients with a good service later, so let's first look at the value of networking and how and why it works.

The value of networking

UHNW individuals are as different as any other group of people, but they have one thing which unites them: wealth.

There are only three things you can do with wealth:

- Invest it.

- Spend it.

- Give it away.

There are advisors for each one of these activities, from shopping consultants to corporate financiers to succession lawyers. Every UHNW will have an advisor of some sort or another.

> Every UHNW will have an advisor of some sort or another.

Wealth needs to be transacted through a bank – so every UHNW individual will have a banker or custodian. Nearly every UHNW will need to pay tax, so nearly all will need a tax advisor or accountant to fill in the annual returns. About 56% have an investment manager, while just 20% are actively engaged with a lawyer at any one time (although most will need to resort to one or more at some time of their lives).

Although UHNW individuals are not easy to identify, and even when identified are difficult to engage, they can all be found through their advisors, and advisors are easy to find. It is hardly surprising therefore that the preferred route to market is networking, but to do it well it needs to be fully understood and put into context.

By setting goals and planning, you will have identified the work and clients that make you the most profit and which sort of business you would like to increase. Now you need to identify the sorts of advisors with the type of client you want that are complementary to what you are doing.

Before we drill into the detail, let us take a look at the difference between old and new money. Old money is the term for when the founder of a fortune, or the next generation, has been brought up by wealthy parents. These people are familiar with wealth ownership. They will know other UHNW individuals; they will have gone to school with them, shot together, gone fishing, hunting, or to the same clubs. If they are troubled by something, they know someone they can call, who can invariably point them in some direction or another – it may not be the right direction, but it will be a start. To make inroads into old money, you will probably need to have gone to the right schools, be good at entertaining, and engage in one or more of the pursuits old money enjoys.

New money is very different. A sheet metal worker called Bob, who built his business into an empire from scratch, will have met people and have his own contacts, but they may not be the right contacts to make the recommendations he needs after he has sold his business. These people when new to liquid wealth are vulnerable; they need to learn, but they will not have the right network to assist them. From my experience, one-third of UHNW individuals lose one-quarter of their wealth within five years of having a liquidity event because they do not know who to trust or who will point them in the right direction.

New money needs communities from which they can learn, like the events for the UHNW community hosted by BConnect Club and their members which was formed to educate, facilitate introductions and find investment opportunities and advisors. New money also needs advisors who care for them and introduce them to their own network of advisors who will help get them to where they want to go.

> New money needs communities from which they can learn...

An advisor needs a network that looks after the type of client he or she wants, and whose services are complementary.

Adrian is a discretionary portfolio manager. He should be looking for a client who has had a 'liquidity event' such as an inheritance, sale of a business, or property portfolio. The types of professionals Adrian needs for his network are private client lawyers, corporate financiers and estate agents.

Once you have identified who you want in your network, you need to:

- Sift out who those you don't want – the time wasters and coffee drinkers – and politely find a group function to keep them up-to-date if you like them. You do not want to spend too much time on them.

- Make a list of who you want and do your homework.

- For those who pass your analysis, tell them you would like them in your network.

- Ask them for examples of the type of work they've done for their clients and the type of clients they have. Ask them for their case studies. If they are reluctant to give them to you, they may also be reluctant to refer any business to you.

- Give them your selection of case studies.

- Find something for them to do to build up the number of 'touches' that are needed before they refer business to you (see below).

A great way to work out which advisors may be interested in what you are doing for your clients is to see who is 'following' you online on BConnect Club or LinkedIn and find out whether what they are doing for their clients is complementary to what you are doing for yours. Filtering online is also the best way to save time that could be far more profitably spent on your clients and chosen network.

What can we learn from professional sales consultants?

Advisors **sell** advice. They are professionals, which means they are being paid to advise. Being a professional does not mean that you are any good. Quite often, advisors are regulated to make sure that they keep up-to-date and do not exploit the vulnerable.

> Only 1-3% of people will be interested in what you do the first time they hear about you.

Regardless of what you are selling, whether it is meat, shoes or advice, only 1-3 % of people will be interested in what you do and the problems you help resolve the first time they hear about your service or product. This means you need to phone fifty people before you get one person who may be ready to hear what you have to say. Cold calling produces a low return because the audience is not receptive. It does not mean that it should not be done, but don't expect a good return immediately. You need to find a way to call again to instigate another 'touch'.

On a first encounter, everyone is asking two questions – "Am I going to like you?" and "Are you looking to take advantage of me?" – this is just innate human wariness about the influence of strangers.

Let's look at "Am I going to like you?" Everyone likes to meet people like them. Have you ever noticed how similarly dressed you and your friends are? And how the body language of a couple engaged in interesting conversation will match each other?

Successful salesmen are trained in Neuro Linguistic Programming (NLP) which teaches the art of rapport: how to adjust your body language, dress and attitude to make the person you are talking to feel at ease. Some salesmen do it well, some not so well.

You will very often see advisors dressing in a similar fashion to their fellow advisors, and you can be fairly sure that they win new business through networking. However, there are some advisors who come from old money; they dress in a similar fashion to their clients and are more likely to win new business direct, whether out shooting or at their club.

Increase the number of touches

Everyone has an innate fear of the influence of strangers or product push. This is why old money likes to win business doing something they enjoy, such as shooting, which gives them the opportunity to meet on several occasions. As they get to know each other, the fear is reduced.

If you are trying to win new business, you need to make sure that your expertise and the problems you help resolve are known by your network; if not, you cannot hope to win business from your network. But how do you get your message across when the person in your network is not interested in your expertise for him or herself, but for their clients?

When trying to win business from a network, not only do you have to overcome the innate fear of the influence of strangers, but you have to convey your message through someone else. From our research, we know that wealth advisors spend 20% of their time prospecting for new business, and of these 42% say they are poor at it, 36% say they are average and only 12% say that they are any good at winning new business.

Whether you are in front of your prospective client or a member of your network, you need five to twelve 'touches' before this innate fear of the influence of strangers is sufficiently suppressed to enable you to influence or sell.

There are four well-worn paths to increasing the number of touches without alerting this innate fear. Each should be woven into your strategy for winning new business:

- Education.

- Aggregation.

- Reciprocation.

- Case studies.

Education

When I was in private practice in Simmons & Simmons, I regularly spoke at conferences. The talks I gave were on my area of expertise and the audience was made up of professionals keen to learn more about what I was doing, but increasingly in Garnham Family Office Services I speak direct to the UHNW community through event oganizers for the UHNW community such as the BConnect Club. Seminars are an excellent way of educating the UHNW community about the problems we can help them resolve. I also write a weekly blog – my Note from Caroline which you get for FREE – see the details at the front of the book.

Education can also be used in 'consultative selling'. This is where you find a topic that is related to your area of expertise that is also something your prospective client may like to find out more about.

As an advisor who is passionate about your area of interest, you have to be very careful. The latest update on the Retail Distribution Review may be riveting to you, but as dull as ditch water to your prospective clients or non- competitor network.

In educating you have to find which level engages your audience and teach them **at that level.**

If your area of expertise is discretionary portfolio management, you may wish to invite an audience of prospective clients from another department to hear about 'seven things you need to know before a liquidity event'. If you are a succession lawyer, you could give a session on 'clogs to clogs in three generations: fact or fiction?'

> You have to find which level engages your audience and teach them at that level.

Education should be focused on what worries your clients or your network, which we call 'Poke the Pain', not on how good you are in your area of expertise. It takes a bit of practice to get to know the difference, but if you are serious about wanting to win new clients, then it is essential to recognise the difference.

David is an investment manager at a bank. He invites three of his network to bring their clients to an evening where his CIO will talk about the current global market trends. David could then invite the same audience to hear an estate agent talk about the housing bubble and a probate lawyer talking about the pitfalls of having real estate abroad. Provided the evenings are not too detailed and boring, education can win new business.

The other factor to bear in mind is that education should not be a one-off. You need to build up the requisite number of 'touches'. Ideally, this is achieved either through a two-day session or a series of eight events.

From our experience, a two-day session takes too much time and patience, so a series of eight events may be better. Remember that it needs to be interactive. Everyone likes to have their say.

Aggregation

The power of aggregation was proved by Benetton. He started out making brightly coloured woolly jumpers that he sold in Italy. He did an experiment, putting a woolly jumper shop in every major street in one town while in another town he put all the shops together on one street. The shops in the latter town sold almost twice the number of woolly jumpers as the other one. This was because people knew that if they wanted a bright red woolly jumper, they could find it on that particular street.

Evidence of the power of aggregation is everywhere. Bond Street is where you go to shop for designer clothes, the farmer's market for local organic fresh food, and Arlington Arcade for cashmere. The power of aggregation is not intuitive unless you understand that people have an innate fear of product push, being sold to or influenced by strangers. However, if there are lots of people selling much the same thing in the same place, this fear is reduced.

It can be seen clearly in the open rate of a newsletter. If sent out from a single organisation the open rate is less than 3%, but if the same articles are sent out from a neutral publisher, the open rate goes up to around 20%. Many wealth advisors say they want exclusivity; in fact, they are more likely to be spotted if they mingle with their competitors in a place where their target market is going to see them.

This is why businesses advertise in magazines and newspapers that are read by their target market. It's also why PR is so effective. If you have a story, a good journalist will write about it and work

> You are more likely to be noticed if you are grouped with your competitors.

in references to your competitors. It is more likely to be read and noticed if you are grouped with your competitors rather than if it were restricted to a piece exclusively about your services. Newspapers and magazines always carry a range of news and views: they know the reader wants to make up her own mind and does not want to have it made up for her.

Sadly, not many wealth advisors use PR because finding an interesting hook and getting the attention of a journalist or editor, who then may not publish the piece, can be expensive with only a modest return. Most wealth advisors therefore choose to network. They go to events where they can find people who have the type of clients they want.

Most wealth advisors have an excellent network, but are not really making it productive. They meet someone at a networking event and within five minutes have established whether or not they have clients that they would like as clients of their own. If they do, they will give them their business card and will probably email them within the next twenty-four hours, suggesting they meet for a coffee. When they meet, they look for areas of mutual interest, share knowledge and then agree when to follow up – if at all.

There are three drawbacks to this method of winning new business:

- **The networking event.** Events come in all shapes and sizes, but before going to an event, you should know why you are going and what it is you want to get out of it. If it is a conference to gain CPD points, it is likely to be full of competitors, so it's unlikely to yield much in the way of people with whom to network to refer business. If an award ceremony, again it will be full of competitors and you will probably be seated with your colleagues and existing network – again, poor for winning new business. If it's a promotion of something or someone, again, the people in the room are probably going to be your competitors, because they see you and your competitors as possible referrers of new business to them. What is needed is an event, where the **sole** purpose is to refer business from professionals who are complementary to what you are doing, for example, conveyancers with estate agents.

- **The lack of useful specific knowledge about what you do for your clients.** If you are a speaker at a conference, you are displaying your specific knowledge to the audience – but the only people really interested in hearing your detailed specific knowledge are likely to be your competitors, who are eager to learn what you know. If you go to these conferences, you are not likely to come across the people you need to meet who can and want to refer business.

- **Traditional networking** on a one-to-one basis, having cups of coffee, takes too much time and is not efficient in follow-up.

Reciprocation

Everyone loves people who care for them, who show an interest in them and who assist them in achieving their goals. Caring means giving and herein lies another conundrum. How can you give and make money?

It comes down to focus. This is why setting goals is so important and should always be done first. Then it is important to identify your target clients or network that has clients who could be interested in your services or products, then evaluate how well you know them – have you 'touched' them sufficiently to start to influence them? If you are not in a position to influence, then you may like to give them something that **they** want – for free preferably something that does not cost you anything more than your time.

Great examples of giving

- **A free one hour consultation.** You could offer this at the end of any case study.

- **A free consultation with the clients of other departments in your organisation.** You could send a case study to your colleagues with this offer at the end of it, or put case studies in your reception or waiting room with an offer of a free consultation at the end of it.

- **A free consultation with the clients of your network.** Again, this could be clearly featured at the end of your news, views or case studies on any aggregation platform, publication or newsletter.

- **Taking in an intern** who could be the daughter or son of a client or member of your network.

- **Making recommendations to your clients**, whether hotels, restaurants, cinemas or trips. For this, you need to keep yourself up-to-date.

- Making introductions to a member of your network.

- **Sharing a case study posted by a member of your network with a client** and telling that member you have done so.

When giving costs money, you need to calculate the return on investment or ROI. Types of giving that have a cost attached are:

- Drinks receptions.

- Meals in restaurants.

- In-house dining; breakfast, lunch, dinner.

- Coffees and teas.

- Events with speakers.

- Christmas cards.

- Books.

- Other token gifts.

It must be very clear before you spend any money why you are doing so and what you want to achieve.

From my experience, too much corporate hospitality is done with no clear aim in mind; just because everyone else spends money on entertaining, you don't necessarily need to follow suit. If money is being spent as a flamboyant gesture, then it will be seen as such, and will win no business. If it is spent with a genuine objective to care for the recipient and to get to know their issues and concerns better, with a positive attitude to resolve any concerns **they** may have as best you can, then it is money well spent and will reap rewards.

Spending money on prospective clients or your network must always be done astutely. There are always people who take and never give. Before and after every expenditure, you need to ask whether it was money well spent. You need to view your contacts and prospects as a gardener tends his garden. Those who always take and never give need to be pruned back and those who are genuine in their efforts to reciprocate need to be nurtured.

Deciding who is a giver and who is a taker should ideally be a collective decision so as to be impartial and commercial without as little personal bias as possible.

Case studies

Probably the most underused and yet best way to win new business is through case studies or telling stories. Everyone loves a story and it is not seen as pushing product. Case studies are 1,227% more likely to be read than an article that has no human content. Of course, it is absolutely essential that the identity of the client is not disclosed, by changing the name, circumstances, age and family situation, and it must not be too convoluted or get bogged down in details. If you follow these rules, case studies are incredibly powerful and completely compliance-friendly.

> Case studies are incredibly powerful and completely compliance-friendly.

If you have acted on all the steps from the beginning, you will know what your best work is and who your best clients are. All you need to do is build a case study around the specific work and type of client you wish to attract and then to publish it.

You could, for example, get a series of ten or twelve case studies from different departments in the office and put them in your reception. Rather than reading the paper while clients are waiting to see a colleague, they could be reading your case studies. If they like what they're reading, they can ask your colleague for an introduction – simple.

You could send this case study compilation to your PR agency to get coverage in the press. Once compiled, it is unlikely to go out of date and so can be used time and time again. If you have any difficulty writing a case study, simply ask a journalist or PR person to do it for you.

Stories are compliance friendly, because you are not pushing product. Tom Burroughs of *Wealth Briefing* and an experienced journalist, says that from his experience, case studies simply 'sizzle off the server' and we have found that as well. A case study is five times more likely to be read than any other news or views.

Simon Brooke, another leading journalist, says that case studies are used by the media; whether speaking on insurance or on Syria, they always want to make it 'come alive' with a story. Charities, politicians and adverts also lean heavily on case studies to gain interest. But to really grab attention, the story should arouse an emotion: lust, sympathy, envy, joy, humour or surprise. It should also include some social proofing. A hotel which asked its guests to re-hang clean towels to be 'kind to the environment' had a response rate of less than 10%. However, when it added 'other guests who have stayed in this room, like you, have re-hung their clean towels', the response rate increased to above 60%! The third element to a good story is a good plot; a hero story, a connection story, a tragedy or a love story, they all maintain interest and take the reader on a journey – what will happen next?

Benefits of a digital platform

Having case studies on a digital platform is enormously powerful for all the reasons listed above.

Education.

- You can read the case studies, news and views of your network.

- They can read yours.

- You can see who is 'following' you.

- You can 'follow' them.

- If you are both 'following' each other, you should consider including that wealth advisor into your network.

- By 'following' you, your UHNW members can filter your news, views and case studies onto their home page, so that they can catch up on tips and traps that they may not otherwise have been aware of.

Aggregation.

- Your network and your UHNW members are attracted to an aggregation platform where they can see a range of professional opinions, news and views.

- The digital platform is neutral and so does not push the products or services of any one provider.

- It is a place where the UHNW knows that she can find expert opinion in a format she can understand.

- The information the UHNW individuals and your network are given can be filtered according to preference.

Reciprocation.

- An article read by a member of your network can be 'liked' to say that this is what their clients are interested in.

- An article read by a UHNW individual can be 'liked' to say 'I want more of this type of article please'.

- An article can be shared with other UHNW individuals.

- An article can be shared with other members of the network or colleagues in different departments.

Case studies.

- Everyone loves case studies – watch the statistics soar.

- Read the case studies of others – the best way to learn.

- Comment on them.

- Enjoy!

We hear a lot of people saying that UHNWs do not use comparison websites, but research by Scorpio, consultants to the UHNW community, revealed that UHNWs are three times more likely to visit a comparison website than any other community, especially if it has something they cannot get elsewhere.

Preparing a campaign

Now you need to work out a campaign and stick to it. The aim of the campaign is to:

- **Be known for the problems you resolve for your clients**. This is not difficult because you know your best clients and your best work from part one.

- **Prepare a series of case studies and education pieces** because we know that these 'sizzle off the server' – everyone loves reading them. Prepare one for every month around your best clients and work. If you have difficulty doing this, use Family Bhive's *Guide to Presenting a Good Case Study*, or ask a journalist or copywriter to write them for you. Make sure you don't reveal any facts that identify the client and make sure you change the names and the details.

- **Schedule these to be featured one every month** on a site that is designed to make online and offline networking efficient and effective.

- **Prepare an email to go to your network.** It should say:

  → I would like you to be in my network as someone to whom I could refer business.

  → I have posted this month's case study online to give you a better idea about the type of problems I resolve for my clients.

  > Case studies 'sizzle off the server' – everyone loves reading them.

  → If you post a case study online, I'll then have a better idea of the problems you resolve for your clients. This will make it easy for me to refer clients to you.

  → Let me know when you have done so because I would like to 'follow' you.

- Say thank you to everyone who 'follows' you.

- Think of something you can give – yes, give – to your network which must be of value **TO THEM, NOT YOU**, so it mustn't be a brochure or anything that is linked to a product push or a sale. As we learned earlier, product push puts people off until such time as you have earned your right to influence. How about a dinner, a speed networking event at your office, or an entertaining speaker instead? No sales pitches, please! Send every member on your list an email with your offer in it.

- As soon as someone in your network posts an education piece or case study, 'follow' it and post a comment to show that you have read it.

- When you meet with anyone on your network, refer to the case study they've posted. This will make them feel you care for them and are thinking about how you can refer business to them.

- Think of clients for whom a case study from your network may be relevant and share it with them. They will love the fact that you are caring for them and thinking of them.

- Regularly review who is 'following' you; look at their case studies, work out if they have clients who could become your best clients for your best work, declare your interest, 'follow' them, and add them to your network list.

- Repeat this every month as each new education piece or case study is featured. It does not matter if you use the same case studies each year because people need to be reminded what sorts of problems you solve for your clients.

- Test which education piece or case study drives the most work and focus on improving the others as you begin to see what works best. Posting on a digital platform gives you valuable feedback about what is working best – something few PR agents are able to do for you.

As you network elsewhere and add more people to your network, remind them that they can see your education pieces and the sorts of problems you resolve for your clients, and direct them to 'follow' you online. In this way, you can be networking even when you're asleep. The time you save, you can profitably spend in caring for your clients.

If you would like to know more about how to get there simply scan the code or copy the link **http://www.garnhamfos.com/wbfpc-extras/ chapter-4-training-material** for some marketing material which will assist you.

Now you know where you want to go, you need to plan as to how you are going to get there, which we cover in the next chapter.

Chapter 5
Trusted Advisors: how to get more clients

Chapter summary:

- Effective corporate literature.

- Using sponsorship wisely.

- How to get ahead with a judicious use of advertising.

- The mysterious world of PR and how to give a good presentation.

- The culture of care in action.

Where have we got to?

In the first chapter, we talked about knowing your best work (i.e. your most profitable work) and who your best clients are. You need to keep focused on this all the time. We delved into planning how to get there in part two, Chapter 4, and then in part three we had a good look at keeping an eye on the time, especially if you're charging by the hour.

In chapter 4 we talked about networking, which is the way most advisors win business, albeit by their own admission 42% of them are poor at it. We also talked

> Is there a golden bullet that will deliver a client time and time again? The short answer is yes – but it takes hard work.

about getting past prospects' innate fear of strangers by increasing the number of 'touches' to the sweet spot between five and twelve, when you can start to influence your prospect or network. You power through this innate fear by using education, aggregation, reciprocation and case studies.

So what have we missed? Is there a golden bullet that will deliver a client time and time again? The short answer is yes – but it takes hard work. In every step we're building on your knowledge so you can reach the point of delivery, which we will deal with in the next chapter.

In this chapter, I want to take you through the other routes to market so that you can decide how best to spend your precious resources.

Two key resources

The most important resources you have are your clients and your network. You must use them wisely. We looked at your network in some detail in the previous chapter (*Getting There*). I want to focus on your current and past clients in the chapter entitled *Retain and Maintain*. But there are other ways you can win business and raise your profile for your services and products.

Corporate literature

A question from the bottom of my heart about corporate literature, whether offline or online, is what are you hoping to achieve? If you don't know, you won't know whether it justifies the cost. If you just want to tell interested parties a little about you and your company, where you're located and who is on your team, that's fine, but it won't win you new business.

If you want to win business, you need to **interest** your network or new prospects with what you can do for them. Please do not copy the corporate literature that's already out there – most of the stuff I've seen does not interest anyone, whether prospects or intermediaries, and should be filed in the bin. However, I am not sure that the purpose of most corporate literature is to interest new prospects or alert your network about the problems you solve. I tend to look at brochures or corporate websites to find more about a particular individual, such as your contact details and where to go for a meeting.

If you refer back to the section on *Aggregation* in the previous chapter, you'll see that most people don't read what is on the website; they are far more likely to go to an aggregation site to find material of interest. This needs to be understood before you can use both your company website and an aggregation site effectively. They use the brochure and website to find out where to go for a meeting, contact details and who is who.

In my view, a corporate brochure or website should be little more than an extended calling card; this is who we are, this is where we are and this is a little to reassure you that we are honest, decent and here for the long haul. None of this information should go on an aggregation platform. There you need to interest your network and client prospects, because they go there to find out what you can do for them – it is here that they go to learn.

You should therefore indicate on all your business cards and corporate literature where clients and prospects can find out what problems you resolve for clients. Don't put these precious gems into your corporate literature because they just won't be seen – **with two massive exceptions**.

- The material you have in your waiting room or reception should be designed to cross-sell your services. It is here that people need to know how you can educate them and what other sorts of problems you can resolve for your clients. Here you should display everything you have prepared for the

> Place corporate literature that cross-sells or up-sells in your reception area. You need to perk people's interest with education pieces...

aggregation platform; the people in your waiting room already know who you are and your contact details.

They **do not need your brochures** when they are sitting in your waiting room. They are already committed to you in some way or they would not be there. This is the time to cross-sell or up-sell, so you need to perk the interest with education pieces or articles about the sorts of problems you resolve for your clients.

The literature in your reception should be in a format that can be taken away and shown to others. It should also have a call to action for them to 'follow' any advisor who is of interest. Remind them about what that advisor does; when they have a problem that advisor can resolve, it will be easy for them to connect.

- After a coffee with someone in your network, by all means give them a brochure, even though you know they probably won't keep it. You need to give them material that will interest them, say one of your education pieces or case studies that direct them to where they can find out more.

Invite them to join your network and 'follow' you. The more 'followers' you have for whom you have contact details, the easier it is to win business from them because they know the calibre of your education and the sorts of problems you resolve for your clients.

Sponsorship

Sponsorship is also a great way to win new business if it's done well. But you must be very clear about what you want to achieve from it. Do you want to:

- Increase brand awareness?

- Increase your network?

- Increase your client prospects?

Increase brand awareness

If it is merely to increase brand awareness, then remember you will only ever interest 1-3% on a product push – so you need to reach a large audience of the right type of people, but you risk being ignored by 97-99%. You'll find out about the benefits of appealing to a large audience in the section on advertising (see below), so I won't repeat it here.

Increase your network

If you want to increase your network, you must make sure that the event attracts the professionals who have clients within your target market.

Furthermore, they need to know what you do for your clients in a way that they can easily share with their clients to enable them to build trust with their clients. We have already talked about how speed networking can do this very effectively especially if done in conjunction with a digital platform to increase the reach of the message and allow networking to continue 24/7.

Increase your client prospects

If you want to increase your client prospects, you need to host an event to which your target market will attend. However, it must be sufficiently intimate to enable you to meet your prospects and sufficiently regular to build a relationship over time. You should therefore find events which are not a one- off, but which interests UHNW individuals such that they will want to attend on a regular basis. Like everyone else, the UHNW want to meet others like them. One brilliant way of asking what event UHNW individuals would like to attend is simply by asking your best clients what they would like to go to and then finding events which they would like. If you are sponsoring events which your best clients would like to go, you will get more people like them and can also invite your clients to them as well thereby building trust.

The basic steps are:

- You need to know whether the event organiser can deliver the audience you want.

- Is the audience interested in the event or merely tolerating the event to meet others with whom to network?

- Will the event organiser build up the requisite five touches before the event?

- How are you going to get your message across to the audience and how is the event organiser going to facilitate this?

- You need to be satisfied that the event organiser can deliver and preferably exceed expectations.

- The event organiser should have an extensive list of people who are the people the sponsor is targeting.

- At the event, the organiser should direct the audience to where it can find the education pieces and the problems that the sponsor resolves. The organiser should urge the audience to 'follow' the sponsor.

- After the event, the event organiser should send an email to everyone on their list directing attention to the sponsor and where email recipients can go to see their education pieces and the sorts of problems the sponsor resolves for their clients.

- Effectiveness can be measured in the increased number of 'followers' who can then be chased up by the relevant advisors.

- The organiser can make introductions and follow up meetings, provided the attendee does not object and can see value in the meeting.

Advertising

What are you hoping to achieve from the advertising campaign? Do you want new business or name awareness, or both? Do you want to appeal to the 1-3% who may be interested in your product or service, or increase the number of 'touches'?

The first and only rule for an advert is that it must be noticed; if not, there is no 'touch' and no increase in brand awareness.

Adverts must:

- **Stand out from the crowd.** We all know that sexy girls in skimpy clothing get noticed. They appeal to the emotion of lust, but appealing to other emotions also works; humour, colour, lack of colour or something odd. Buy a magazine or newspaper and look at the ads that grab your attention. What works and what underwhelms you?

  In the *Financial Times*, one advert I looked at from a wealth manager selling wealth showed a picture of a bug, and another was just orange words on a blue background! What has that got to do with managing money? Where is the emotion, the story, the plot?

- **Good strapline.** Look at the ads again. You'll be amazed at how much money is spent on buying space which means nothing to the reader. The strapline to the ad with the bug was about missing opportunities: did that mean the bird had missed a tasty bug, or that the bug was an opportunity? Rather than focus on the features of the wealth manager, the advert should focus on the clients they are hoping to attract. What is actually worrying clients? If their investments are their only means of income, they want to be sure they are safe – they care little about missed opportunities. If they didn't know they were there, so what?

Fifty-six per cent of people who use a wealth manager (according to Scorpio) are risk averse. What does this tell us? They don't care about missing an opportunity; they want a professional to manage their money. What they want is

> Adverts should focus on the clients they are hoping to attract. What is actually worrying clients?

to sleep at night knowing their money is in safe hands. They want a wealth manager who cares about them and their concerns.

- **Body copy.** Most adverts I looked at in this particular copy of the *Financial Times* made a lot of predictions such as 'We believe the crisis on the Continent is over' or 'We find the potential others miss'. Can they live up to these claims? I'll be addressing this in the next chapter, because most cannot. If wealth managers confidently assert things they cannot deliver, the real message that will be taken away is 'I cannot trust you'. If you're hoping to attract a risk averse audience, this is just the message that will put them off!

  Almost all of the adverts then went on to talk about how long they'd been in business and how many analysts they have engaged worldwide. What a waste of space and precious resources. The reader wants to know what the advisor can do for me, not how many mouths his money will be feeding.

  An advert should be a condensed case study. If the adverts focused on the client's concerns and the ways they go about resolving them, they would genuinely create increased brand awareness which can then be measured by an increased number of leads.

- **Call to action.** Going back to the adverts in the *Financial Times*, I was shocked to see that one had no call to action! How on earth is this wealth advisor going to win new business with no call to action? Three others had what looked like telephone numbers from a call centre and several others instructed the reader to go to their website. If you went to the websites as directed, there would be no easy way for the organisation to capture these contact details, so the lead would have no option but to go cold.

The marketing directors of each and every advert I looked at should be held to account. They are spending the company's precious resources and if adverts don't result in increased lead generation and sales, what is their value?

I'm not negative about advertising, just advertising that is done badly. If done well, it can generate a massive increase in interest and leads, but the adverts must adopt a culture of care to be effective: they need to be client-focused, not a glorified ego trip, and they need to **capture data on which a follow up can be made**.

Advertising, if done well, should not be limited to print media; it could be complemented with billboard, radio, TV, direct mail, online platforms and cable, once you know that something is working.

Public relations

Some people are terrified of dealing with the press, although they shouldn't be. What everyone needs to understand is that a journalist is doing a job, which is to write stories that their readers will enjoy and that will sell the newspaper. As more people buy or take the publication, so the cost of advertising space goes up.

Bearing in mind what we have said in the previous chapter about the innate fear everyone has of product push and how we get around this with education, aggregation, reciprocation and case studies, it becomes easy to work out what the journalist is looking for in a press release.

> If a press release is educational, or talks about solving a problem for a client, it is infinitely more likely to be picked up by both journalist and reader.

If you prepare a press release with nothing more than the features of your new product or service, it may get noticed because the newspaper is in effect an aggregating platform. However, if is educational, or talks about solving a problem for a client, it is infinitely more likely to be picked up, not only by the journalist, but also by the reader.

The great advantage of using a PR agent rather than trying to do it yourself is that they have personal connections with the journalists and editors and know what makes a good story. It is absolutely imperative if you are to use

PR that you recognise what a reader is going to do once they have read about you. They will probably go to your website to find out more.

As I've said above, the website should clearly show who you are, your contact details and that you are around for the long term, but **most importantly** it needs to capture **their contact details**.

If you'd like to know more about us, call (and then give someone's name); or click here (which must lead to a page where you can **capture their email address**). **If** you don't, you will have lost all the benefit of the good PR.

Every press release sent to a journalist should be followed by a call. Once you have a comment in the press, use or quote from it. Make sure you use it as a flyer in your reception area, as an article you can promote on the Internet, and have your colleagues send it out to their clients or network. Once you have it, flaunt it; it is invaluable third-party endorsement!

Speaking at conferences

If you are going to speak at a conference, let your network know; ask if they would like to see the slides or the transcript and let them know where and when you will be speaking.

A speaking slot can be an opportunity to win new business or it can be a bore, and it all boils down to the same principles – a culture of care. You'll be talking to human beings who have their own goals and if you can assist them in winning their goals, not only will they listen and learn, but they'll want to add you to their network too.

The talk therefore needs to be **interesting**, which means educational with case studies. Again, when I say interesting, I mean interesting to the audience, not the speaker. A good way to start is to reduce what you are trying to communicate down to a case study.

> The talk needs to be interesting... and I mean **interesting** to the audience, not the speaker.

Let's say you were talking about the new tax legislation to be introduced on holiday lets. It's easy to start with the title of the legislation and then to go through the various clauses, but that is boring. Make it come alive. Think of someone to whom this legislation may be relevant, and give that person a name and a bit of detail, so people can relate to him as a person.

David is married to Susan and they have two young children, Angus and Jodie. Following the death of David's father, they inherited a bit of money and bought a delightful cottage near Salcombe in Devon which they let out as a holiday let, although they use it for themselves two weeks of the year and at weekends in the winter.

The new legislation that is due to come out in [whenever] will affect David and Susan in the following ways, and our recommendation is that they do x, y, and z to make sure they are compliant.

At the conference, you'll need to have some slides. Visual aids are really important. Eighty-five percent of information is memorised because it was seen rather than heard. People at conferences tend to lose concentration and the slide prompts them on where the speaker has got to. It allows them to catch up. Colour is extremely effective, because it excites.

Pictures of people are of most interest. In the above conference, you'll need a picture of David and Susan with their children, either outside their cottage in Devon or on the beach in Salcombe. There are so many images you can buy, so you can easily find a good photo that illustrates your case study.

The use of visuals will greatly enhance the expectations of the audience and illustrations with people and stories will greatly improve their memory of it.

Personal contact

For wealth advisors, your primary contacts are going to be with your network. In the previous chapters, we worked on how to build a strong network that has clients who you know are of a type that could become your best clients and for your best work. You now need to create a strategy of how to communicate with your network in a way that will deliver the referrals you are looking for.

Make your network feel special

- **Make your network feel special**. You want your network to refer business to you and not to anyone else, so you need to make them feel special, which is again part of our culture of care. They are trying to win business from you so recognise that. Make sure you are following them and read their case studies and education pieces. When you meet them, refer to what they've published. Make sure you've given them something of value that is not your product, brochure or a speech by your CEO. How about making it fun by giving them boat trips, speed networking, or special events?

- **Ask open questions**. Show your network you care for them, their families, work difficulties and challenges. An open question leads to a discussion and the more personal it is (within the confines of decency), the better. How long have you been working for [x]? Where were you before and what do you like about [x]?

- **Work should not be all work and no play**. There is no reason why you shouldn't have a joke with members of your network who appreciate your humour.

- **Care for your network**. If they look sad, ask them what's the matter and if they look joyful, you can ask them what there is to celebrate; empathise with them and commiserate with them.

- **Do you share common interests?** Do you support the same football team, enjoy cricket or love food? Find common interests and bring these up at every opportunity.

- **Keep a record of all the above**. You need to record small details such as the names of their children and wife, the name of their dog, or which pub they go to. Bringing up these small details shows you care – and a culture of care wins business.

For reciprocation to work:

- You must be willing to refer your clients to your network.

- This is not something you should be embarrassed about.

- **Clients *like* their advisors to care for them** and, if done in a friendly and subtle way, should bind the client closer, not drive them away.

- **Sharing case studies with a client saying "I thought this may be of interest to you or one of your friends,"** shows you care for your client; you stay in touch and find out more about them which puts you in a better position to up-sell or cross-sell.

- **Sharing case studies with your clients** gives you an opportunity to stay in touch, so that they are less inclined to go with any other advisor and more likely to trust you.

- **Make sure your network knows** that you have clients in your gift to refer to them, but that you're not going to refer work to members of your network who do not reciprocate or care for their clients in a similar way.

> Make sure your clients know you're sharing your network's services with them because *you care for them.*

- **Make sure your clients know** you're sharing your network's services with them, not for any monetary gain (unless there is, in which case you need to be totally transparent), but because you care for them. They will reward you handsomely.

In the next chapter, I'll be taking you through how to deliver; turning up the heat, dealing with objections, and closing. Don't forget UHNWs need advisors to avoid making losses, find opportunities and stay compliant. As you will have seen from previous chapters, it is incredibly hard for them to find the advisors they need and, if you can assist them with this, they will be eternally grateful.

Chapter 6
The Trusted Advisor: delivery

Chapter summary:

- Selling to the right brain.

- Features and benefits and how to use them.

- Always talk your audience's language.

- Winning new business: from first meeting to point of sale.

- Don't be shy: ask for the business.

Human behaviour

Psychology is the study of human behaviour and how it reacts to stimuli. Malcolm Gladwell's book *The Tipping Point* talks about social psychologist Howard Levanthal's experiments on fear. He put together seven booklets ranging in intensity of severity on tetanus with a call to action to go to the campus clinic to be immunised for free.

Only 3% of students who were given the booklet went to the health centre to get an injection, **regardless of the intensity of the fear** in the booklets. He did the test again, this time including a map showing where the clinic was and the opening times, even though most students were familiar with the clinic. The number of students who took the jab after the second distribution went up to 28% regardless of the level of fear in the booklet. Howard put this down to the fact that when the decision was made easier for them, more students took the jab.

If you look at the results through the eyes of a sales consultant, every human has an innate fear of the influence of strangers and regardless of what is being offered, only 1-3% will take it up.

To the rational left brain, taking a tetanus jab is a no-brainer; it could make the difference between life and death. But the right brain says, "Beware of strangers". When presented a second time with a clear picture of the clinic and its opening times, which every student was already familiar with, the innate fear of the influence of strangers was reduced. Naturally, the take-up was higher.

If rational, left brain thinking was a driver of decisions, then the students reading the higher intensity of fear booklets would have correlated to the immunisation take-up, but there was no correlation; decisions were not being made on a left brain basis.

If we want to influence others to use our services or buy our products, we need to appeal to their right brain, their emotional brain, and only if manifestly wrong or right will the left brain, the rational mind, be brought in to review the situation. Once this is understood, everything else falls neatly into place.

Features and value

Every wealth advisor or advisor to a UHNW individual (or indeed anyone) needs to know the difference between benefits and features. Features are the facts about a service or product while a benefit is how it will resolve their concerns or issues. A salesman in a dress shop may say, "Madam, look at the quality of the finish on this dress". This is a feature. If he says, "All eyes will be

> Right brain thinking cares little for the absolute outcome; it is more influenced by someone who is seen to care for them, their issues and concerns.

on you when you wear this dress," that is a benefit (if the client wants to draw attention to herself).

Left brained thinking is about identifying what the issues and concerns of the client are, right brained thinking deals with the features of the service and products. Extraordinary as it may seem, even though in our everyday life we tend to display more right brain behaviour, we are taught from an early age to describe what we do with left brain analysis.

Gordon is a wealth manager. When asked what he does by a colleague, he may say, "I manage my client's money, making sure we return upper quartile performance for them". However, if you asked one of his clients they may say, "I like Gordon. He does a good job; he always calls me back and is there to reassure me if the economy looks as if it is going to crash."

Right brain thinking cares little for the absolute outcome; it is more influenced by someone who is seen to care for them, their issues and concerns. Clearly, Gordon's client is interested in someone returning his calls and being able to sleep at night when the economy looks as if it is going to crash. If Gordon were to invite his client to lunch and tell them how well they had responded compared to the benchmark, it would bore them. However, if Gordon found out that his client's daughter was going to Harvard for a year and he was able to share an article on tax breaks for foreign students going to the US, his client would be delighted. He'd see Gordon as caring for him, and that would boost the trust between them.

The right brain responds to emotion; excitement, colour, warmth, love and being made to feel special. In short, we all want other human beings to care for us and unless something is manifestly wrong or right, a feeling of security is often more important than getting the best deal.

This is where education is so important. The UHNW individual has to have some knowledge before they'll know whether something **is** manifestly right or wrong. They have to ask questions from time to time, for fear of trusting blindly and being led away from their goals towards the goals of their advisors – no matter how well intended they may be.

To summarise, we all have an innate fear of being influenced by strangers and no matter how compelling the proposition, our decisions aren't based on rational thought. The primary driver is an emotional response. If we were driven by logic, we'd be influenced by features. But we are not; we are far more influenced by benefits and our emotions. It is therefore extremely important to know the difference between benefits and features. Learn to focus on the benefits for your clients when working on winning new business.

Examples of features would be:

- The continual education of our lawyers. Clients expect their lawyer to be up to date with the law so that's not a great benefit!

- We have offices in all major continents.

- Analysts to cover all investment types.

- A soldier looking after your personal safety.

- Bright new offices.

- We've been in business for more than one hundred years.

- Our fund was voted best for 2013.

For an estate agent, a benefit would be, "We want to find your dream house," while a feature would be, "We have 430 houses on our database". For an accountant, "We deal with the tedium of wealth leaving you free to enjoy it," is a benefit, while "All our accountants are made to do 54 hours of education a year to ensure they are up-to-date with all the latest news and views," is a feature.

The elephant in the room is, what are the concerns and worries of the client?

The salesman in the boutique has assumed the lady in the dress wants all eyes on her, but the client may be desperately shy or a celebrity and want to fade into the background. Making assumptions about what people want is always risky.

You can, of course, ask your clients. This is known as market research. It will give you a better guess about what the audience wants. At some point, however, you will still have to test and see what works and try something different to see if that works any better. If you divide your clients into two groups and try one form of wording on one and another form of wording on another, that is called split testing.

You may say to group one, "We manage your money so that you can enjoy it," and to group two "We manage your money so that you can sleep at night," and see which produces the better return. The joy of doing split testing on a digital platform rather than through advertising or PR, is that you can see precisely who's reading the article and how many, so the results are instantaneous. Once you have the response, then the advertising campaign or PR can be adjusted accordingly.

Marketeers

Marketeers are the experts who identify the benefits of a product and refine the sales message to produce the maximum impact. Let's assume you've worked out through split testing that "We take the tedium out of your wealth so you can enjoy it," works best with a select audience. A marketeer will then tweak and refine it to find out how best to communicate it to your audience; changing the wording, positioning and pricing to see what has the greatest impact.

A marketeer is looking for mini trends within the selling process that may not be obvious, but subtle differences can make a significant difference to the take-up of a product or service.

If you are a succession lawyer and your benefit is "We make sure your loved ones are cared for when you are not there to do so," you may like to split an invitation to your seminar into two groups:

- Group 1   A picture of a loving family.

- Group 2   A picture of a grieving family at a funeral. Is there a significant difference in response?

Numerous studies have shown that putting a number in the text always gets a higher response. For example:

- Group 1   5 things to do before you die.

- Group 2   May you rest in peace.

Curiosity in the strapline also produces significantly higher results, such as, "Wasn't it weird?"

But, although there are degrees and books and study courses on marketing, until anything you do is tested, it remains a hypothesis. We are dealing with people and they are fickle at best and influenced by events and others over which we have no control at worst.

Being flippant can backfire

Gerald Ratner famously lost a business and a fortune for likening his jewellery to a prawn sandwich. I'm sure he meant to be funny, but one little slip and his life was ruined. I was chairing a speed networking panel where one of the panelists had prepared an excellent case study. He had the audience enthralled until he mentioned the bank from whom he had won the new business. Instantly, his credibility nosedived. It always pays to care and respect the competition if you want to win credibility. His audience was his network and there were people in the audience from that organisation. Business is not won by treading on the toes of your competitors.

Similarly, it is important to know who you want as clients and focus on them alone. To take an example from *The Tipping Point*, the makers of the programme *Sesame Street* wanted to appeal to both adults and children so that adults could be engaged with the education of their children. It was a sensible rational proposition, but it didn't work.

> It is important to know who you want as clients and focus on them alone.

One joke designed for the adults was a pun on princesses in distress, Kermit said, "Excuse me, are you a female princess in distress?" to which the princess replied, "What does it look like? A pant suit?" This was funny to the adults, but was lost on the preschool child and from that point was easily distracted. When the children didn't understand some aspect of the programme, it lost their attention.

Blue Clues, on the other hand, relied solely on the child's attentiveness. For adults, the programme was a plodding, literal show that was repeated five times in a row. It was boring for adults because it was too slow for them, but the children loved it and their learning rate and attention soared.

When I was a child, my mother used to read Winnie the Pooh stories to me and my sister at bedtime. Both my sister and I recall occasions when our mother would literally be wiping tears from her eyes, but for us children all we can remember is that her nose vibrated as she laughed – the jokes were completely lost on us.

This tells us a lot about left brain activity and education. After the emotional innate fear is suppressed with familiarity, left brain activity wants to engage. It is inquisitive, but will switch off the moment it is bored, or finds the information irrelevant or too difficult.

After we've become familiar to our buyer or referrer, we now need to interest them without putting them off. Humans like to learn about matters that resolve a concern or worry they have. Learning or education must therefore be interesting **to them**, which means the information must not be something they know already or something that is too difficult. It should not be a product push, which will again arouse their innate fear, unless the product push is amongst many others on an aggregation platform. To maintain their interest, it must be relevant to them, which means it is resolving a concern or worry of theirs, and it must be pitched at their level, taking them one small step forward, neither too little nor too large.

We all like to think that brilliant ideas come out of the brains of brilliant people, but in reality most successes come out of trial and error, learning some basic facts about what people want and how they behave, and a lot of hard work refining the product and sales message. Assumptions are just that, good ideas, but until tested as to what the market wants, they will not lead to a profit, which is the core of any business.

Point of sale

In Chapter 2 we were reminded that UHNW individuals want their advisors to care for them, they want them to point out opportunities and traps. One way of doing this is to share the case studies, news and views of your carefully chosen network with them, gently asking them whether what they have read could be of interest. Networking by sharing news, views and case studies with clients provides qualified leads for the case study shared, which then needs to be converted into clients.

George is a banker who has won numerous clients by providing short term borrowings on the security of real estate. He produces an excellent case study. Lucy is a tax lawyer whose client Jeffrey is due to sell his house to relocate to London, but is struggling to make ends meet in the interim. She shares George's case study with Jeffrey, who is delighted that Lucy cares for him to the extent that she has been able to propose a solution. Lucy arranges an introduction between Jeffrey and George. A week later, she arranges to meet George for a coffee and reminds him that he may like to reciprocate the favour. Now he will be looking out to win new business for Lucy because she did a favour for him for free – she is now looking to him to reciprocate.

If you are serious about winning new business from your network, you should not assume that there are people out there like Lucy who will think of you when they are working with their clients. You need to increase the likelihood of them referring business to you.

> Your goal is to increase the likelihood of your network sharing your case studies with their clients.

Let's assume you're an expert on business property inheritance tax relief and you have written a case study that you have shown to your network. Your network may or may not have shared it with their clients, so your goal is to increase the likelihood of them doing so. You have a goal, now you need a plan. An education seminar is prepared and a date and venue.

Arrange to meet your network one by one armed with a plan of action and some carefully thought out questions. You start off with David. David has posted some interesting views on EIS investments that you have read by way of homework.

When you meet David, you could start off by discussing EIS investments. Then you want to bring the conversation around to your seminar on '5 things you need to think about before you die'. You must be armed with some interesting non-threatening facts.

"Did you know that 78% of entrepreneurs aged 50 or over have made no succession plans?" You could continue the discussion along these lines until you say something like, "I'm holding an event for entrepreneurs in six weeks time. It's called '5 things you need to think about before you die'. Do you have any entrepreneurs as clients? Perhaps you could bring five of them with you."

Make your request specific.

Now you need to be armed with answers to all the possible objections: "We don't have a programme for our clients."

- "Why not? We ran an event with X [a competitor]. We met his clients and they met ours and they loved it. You wouldn't want X getting all our clients would you?"

- "How do you win new business?"

- "What are your targets for this year?"

- "Do you struggle to win new business?"

- "Does your organisation assist you with any training?"

This series of questions is designed to intensify their need to bring their clients to your event because they will get a chance meet with your clients.

First meeting

When it comes to the event it must be **educational**, not a product push. It must be full of interesting facts and case studies. You must do what you can to engage and interest – a product push will be resisted and put the audience off.

> The event must be educational, not a product push. It must be full of interesting facts and case studies.

The aim for the first event is to do nothing more than generate a lead and a few answers on the feedback form to questions like, "How relevant was the topic for you?" Then you need to keep the lead warm with a series of emails, all of which are interesting and informative (no product push), and a telephone call to ask for feedback. Don't try to make a sale at this stage, wait until the prospect is really warm. You have already given them an opportunity to learn; you may like to think of what else you can give them that could be of value to them.

When the time is right, and not before at least five touches, which are all about them, not you, you may suggest a meeting. Let's say David has introduced you to Alex and Alex agrees to meet you.

You could start by addressing any open questions. "On the feedback form, you said our event was 'highly relevant'. Am I right in assuming you are an entrepreneur?"

See where the conversation goes, but be mindful about the questions you need to ask and in particular any killer issues.

For inheritance tax to be of any importance, you need to establish what his business is and whether it will qualify. You'll need to know his family circumstances; if he doesn't have heirs, he may care little about tax on death, or if he wants to give it all away to charity, he may have little concern about inheritance tax.

After all your pre-set boxes have been ticked, you need to steer the conversation around to your elevator pitch, which must focus on the benefit to your prospect, not on any features. Remember, you know your prospect reasonably well by now, you have already met in a neutral setting and engaged with him in several non-threatening ways; you now need to get to the point, and there is no doubt that your prospect will want you to.

"Are your loved ones well provided for if anything were to happen to you?" You have to be armed with questions to any answers like, "I already have a plan in place." You need to have a reply in mind: "When was the last time it was reviewed? Did you know the law changed in x?"

He may say, "We have always used x for our succession planning." You must have a reply to this too. You could say, "X is really good, I've worked with him before, but would you welcome a fresh pair of eyes to review what he's done? After all, you want your loved ones to have the best possible plan for when you are no longer there to look after them."

If a prospect is keen to come to your seminars, but seems deaf to engaging with your services or products in a commercial manner, you need to find out why – it is rarely to do with a lack of funds. You need to find out what the objections are.

It may be an irrational fear that once they have done a succession plan that death will be around the corner – it's daft, but you need to unearth the objection to flush it out. It may be that they have had the same advisor for many years and are reluctant to switch.

At this stage, may I remind you **never say anything derogatory about your competitors;** it is a small world and bad mouthing the competition soon gets out and will come back to bite you.

You may not win business straight away. If that's the case, you must leave your prospect with something on which you can follow up.

"May I give you a case study on a client who sounds very similar to you? You really should have your arrangements independently reviewed from time to time, and if there is nothing further to add, we'll only charge for the review and nothing more."

Qualifying buyers

In the example given above, our advisor is dealing with a highly qualified lead. Alex is a client of David, who will already know a lot about him. He has indicated on the feedback form that the talk was 'highly relevant' and he has given you his contact details and opened your emails.

Talented sales people will qualify a lead in every way possible before they start the "This is what I can do for you" spiel because it is at this stage that (if the buyer is not willing) the innate fear will pop up, they will go cold, and all your hard work will have come to nothing.

On the flip side, in the example given above, if the sales pitch is not made, there is a real danger that all your hard work will arouse interest in Alex, but rather than give the work to you, he'll return to his existing succession lawyer. It is not dissimilar to dating. A guy will woo his lady with flowers and a dinner, but at some stage he needs to display his affection or he faces losing her to someone else. He will have been nothing more than a teaser.

I have had the dubious pleasure of watching a stallion at work. The mare is aroused by some lesser male, the 'teaser', who is then led away to be replaced by the stallion.

By not showing an interest in wanting to work for your prospect, you are leaving the door open for someone else to benefit from your hard work. Don't be cross if someone benefits from you not asking for the work: you had your chance and missed it. Learn from your mistake and make sure that next time, you don't miss out.

One objection to a sales pitch could be, "Yes, I can see a review would be nice to have, but I really don't have the budget at the moment." Don't be annoyed or irritated by objections; they are opportunities to learn. To take this a stage further, you need to find out more.

"If money were no object, would you want a review?" This type of question is aimed at flushing out whether this is the only objection or one of many. If the client says yes then we can look at financing the review, a payment plan or whatever.

However, for UHNW individuals, funds are rarely going to be a problem, so flushing out the real objections is key.

"I have been with my tax advisor for five years and he has all my papers. I don't know how you can do a review without passing over his files." At this stage, all you now need to say is, "He must have sent you a report summarising his advice and your situation. I don't need to see his files, just that report, and I can take it from there."

Alex is nearly a client, but you could lose him at this stage, because his commitment is weak.

A quick and smooth follow up is important

If you have had a good presentation or meeting with a prospect, a smooth and quick follow up is essential. All the hard work done to date can be completely wasted by not following up quickly or smoothly.

Enthusiasm is contagious. At a presentation, your audience is a crowd and will behave like a crowd, they will take their lead from others, and if there is a general feeling of goodwill and positive energy, they will feel it and want to remain a part of it. But when they are no longer part of the crowd, some doubts or worries may start to crawl back in

> ...when they are no longer part of the crowd, some doubts may crawl back in from their reticular activating system...

from their reticular activating system and the innate fear of influence of strangers. Similarly, if you have had a good one-on-one meeting, your prospect will have felt the warm glow of your undivided attention. Though it felt good at the time, when he's alone doubts may start creeping in.

Until you have won a sale, it is not a sale. You need to maintain the same level of interest, attention to detail and contact, but maintain the human interaction as much as possible. If someone is not buying, and the product or service has a genuine benefit for them, the innate fear has not been reduced sufficiently to make them want to buy from you, so increase the 'touches'.

Continue to emphasise the benefits and continue to care.

Price

Marketeers talk a lot about the 'price point'; if you lower the price, you'll get more buyers and if you increase the price, you'll sell less. The exception to this rule is at the luxury end. Hermès never discounts its stock in the shop because its customers do not want their scarves and ties to be worn by people who will only buy in a sale. They want the brand to remain exclusive – available only to UHNW individuals. I have covered this in greater detail in the chapter on Retaining and Maintaining a trusted relationship.

In the previous example, our advisor has persuaded Alex to give him the report that was prepared a few years ago on business property relief. Alex feels good about it, but now our advisor must build on this nice feeling.

What do supermarkets do to make their customers buy? First it is never really about the price. Even in supermarkets that are not full of UHNWs, there are only a few people checking out the price. The price is a left brained response and as we know the first response is rarely a rational one. People like to treat themselves. It makes them feel special. They want something that 'catches their eye'. This makes the supermarket experience sticky and makes the customer want to come back.

Different supermarkets appeal to different customers, and the supermarkets need to know what a 'treat' is for their customers and how to attract their customers to it.

- Buy one get one free.

- Buy **now** while stocks last.

- If you like that, you may like this.

- Money back guarantee if not totally satisfied.

- Special displays.

- Because you are a loyal customer, you may like this.

- Special offer until Sunday.

- Positioning on a shelf.

These tricks are not restricted to supermarkets; they work because people like them whether they are buying luxury goods or washing powder.

In selling, psychological tests have shown that the moment someone has made a decision, their reticular activating system starts justifying why it was the right thing to do, and this endorsement makes them feel good. This is the moment that a client is most receptive to an up-sell.

If you buy one item, luxury brands will give you a gift or they'll offer to send you a brochure of the new season's collection. When you buy some shoes, the salesperson will show you the bag that goes with them, and they may invite you to a fashion show if you buy the bag as well. It is human behaviour they are playing with and it works.

Advisors, as a general rule, do not give their clients anything like the same attention and care as the luxury brands, but more about this in the next chapter.

Remember the following tips

It is the personal contact that most people want, because people buy from people. You have, however, got to make it easy to follow up. The following tips will help:

- **Get to know your contacts**. Do they have children doing exams, running a marathon, or due to go into hospital? Make a note and phone them.

- to find out how it went. What are their goals; can you help them with anything, make an introduction, do something together? Through these links, you are building bonds.

- **Can you genuinely provide value for them?** Do you know enough about them to provide value for them through your services and products?

- If not, what is it you need to know to assist them in their goals thereby building trust.

- **How can you make your services and products appear more valuable to them?** Do you have testimonials, press coverage, or recommendations from respected advisors that you can add to your case studies to make your service of more value to them? This is social proofing and it makes your advice appear more valuable in the eyes of the client. Can you give them any form of guarantee which will ease their fears? Guarantees are also a great way of reducing the fear of making a bad decision.

- **Can you create any urgency?** What will the result be if they don't use your services? Will they have sleepless nights, risk family harmony on their death, or a dissipation of their assets over time? Or will they lose out to competitors, lose clients, miss out on opportunities, fail to make their targets? Is there anything they need to do NOW?

- **What objections do they still have and have you flushed them all out?** Ask them what's holding them back or causing the delay. If you have built a good relationship, they should tell you, they won't allow you to continue to pester them if they want nothing from you. If they have a genuine reason, fine; simply make an appointment for a better time.

- **Close.** This is when they finally cross the line. What was it that clinched it? Remember it, because you may need to use it again.

How to deal with your prospects and core network

In your dealings with new prospects and your core network, always:

- **Be open and transparent.** No one is going to respond to someone who appears to have something to hide, is evading answers, or is more keen to see someone on the other side of the room. If you are in a room with someone and you are genuinely looking out for someone, say so and why. You must not give the impression that you're not interested. Similarly, if you need to make a call at a specific time or you have a meeting immediately afterwards say so, so that when you look at your watch, it is not taken as a gesture of being bored.

- **Be honest.** Don't lie. There is a great expression 'What a tangled web we weave, when first we practice to deceive'. People eventually work out who is deceptive because they cannot keep up with their lies. Salespeople I have come across often say that exaggeration is not a lie. However, if you are found out as having deliberately exaggerated, your reputation will suffer with everyone who hears the gossip.

- **Mean what you say.** If you say you're going to send an email today, make sure you send that email today and not tomorrow. If you cannot, say so, but don't make a habit of making excuses.

- **Be punctual.** It is disrespectful to be late. Other people don't have time to waste and you should not be wasting their time.

- **Know what it says in your contract** and point out the things they need to know.

- **Be honest about what they can expect** as a client and what level of reporting they will get.

- **Refuse to compromise yourself.** A client is not worth having at any cost.

One final word...

When you play tennis, you choose a tennis court and make sure that your opponent knows the rules of the game. Imagine what the game would be like with no lines and no proper understanding of the rules. It wouldn't be a game worth playing. You'd be constantly arguing about what was in and what was out and who was winning and what the score was.

However, so many advisors rush into giving advice without a proper understanding about the terms of engagement. So why are they surprised when there is so much disagreement and disputes about payment of the fees? Do not engage without a proper understanding about the terms of engagement, but more about this in Chapter 7.

If you would like to know more, about how to deliver simply scan the code or copy the link **http://www.garnhamfos.com/wbfpc-extras/ chapter-6-training-material** for training material which will assist you.

Now you know how to deliver, you need to maintain and retain your client which we cover in the next chapter.

Chapter 7
Retain and maintain: advisors

Chapter summary:

- Good client service is essential.
- Think beyond the business and serve clients as best you can.
- Increasing profits.
- Up-selling and cross-selling.
- Build your brand: from Ugly Sister to princess.

Up until now, most of this book has been about winning new business, which is important. But possibly of greater importance is appreciating the value of the customers you already have. Not only do they pay your bills, salaries, and bonus, but as we have seen in the previous chapter, they are your ticket to winning new business. In Chapter 3, we focused our attention on time management. You need to use the time you've saved for your clients, to learn about their issues and concerns, and to assist them wherever you can. If you focus your efforts on trying to assist your clients, you will focus on building your network with advisors they may want to know and making introductions as and when appropriate. You will then easily grow your business with good and profitable work.

Your best clients are therefore **your most valuable asset.** You need to understand this and treat them as such. Taking advice is for many a distressed purchase, a bit like going to the dentist. You need to pay your taxes and to make arrangements for your death, but just as your dentist could make your visit a pleasure, so you must aim to make your clients trust you and to turn a pain into a pleasure.

Try to put yourself in the shoes of your clients. What would you like if you were seeking advice?

The value of good service

I have served on a number of boards that decide on the winners of awards, but probably the most interesting was the *Investor's Chronicle* board of award winners. The board is very small because they base their award on what the public says and not on what their fellow advisors think. The highest score in each category is always awarded to the organisation that provides the best quality of service – not on performance. We are human; our choices are often made using our right brain, not our left. We want our advisor to care for us and provide a good service.

I define service as anticipating a need and providing a solution without being asked. A butler overhears his master telling his dog they'll have a good afternoon. He anticipates that his master wants to go shooting and prepares his gun for him. The butler has anticipated what his master wants and provided the solution, the gun, without being asked.

Are you anticipating your clients' needs and providing a solution without being asked? If your bills are paid quickly, then you probably are.

When I was practicing law, I was always keen to see which of my team had the highest 'lock up' days. This is the term used for how quickly a client paid his bill. Even though it was clear from the terms of engagement that a client needed to pay within fourteen days, very often bills were not settled for six months or more.

This must not be tolerated in any business. If a service has been rendered and the client has received value, then this should be paid for.

If the client does not pay within the time agreed, the advisor needs to know why.

Is it because the client has:

	but knows s/he need not pay on time?
Had good service and good advice	
	but knows the price is negotiable?
Had good advice, but the service was poor?	
Had good service, but the advice was poor?	
	and is reluctant to pay?
Not had good service or advice	
	and would like a reduction on the price?

Providing a feedback form with every invoice not only provides you with valuable information, but also acts as a healthy reminder that if the service and advice provided was good, then it should be paid for. If however, the service or advice was poor, this discussion should be had sooner rather than later. You can then negotiate a settlement, learn and move on without impeding cash flows.

A business that is not paid for work done on time needs to borrow to fund the cash flow. Late payment of bills can add up to a serious sum of money. Wealth advisors must not allow their clients to use them as a bank for cheap credit.

> Whatever the value is for the client for advice – it needs to be paid for and paid on time.

A wealth advisor who has a good relationship with a client and provides good advice must always be aware that a client is not a friend. He or she is employed to provide advice that needs to be paid for. The wealth advisor must learn to see the value of this advice and service for his or her client. Can the client sleep at night knowing that her wealth is being managed 24/7?

Are they providing for their loved ones at a time when they will not be there to look after them? Whatever the value is for the client for advice – it needs to be paid for and paid on time.

Using your good relationship to good effect

Clients value good service more than good advice. The secret of providing a good service is knowing what your clients want, giving it to them and then exceeding expectations. For this to work, you need to engage with your client. If you are charging for every minute you get in touch with your client, you'll never know enough about him or her to provide a good service. This is why we took such trouble in Chapter 3 to learn when we are wasting time, so as to free up time to spend with clients without charging. This is not time wasted, it is the most valuable thing you can do for your business. You need to find ways in which you can get to know them without annoying them. Having dinners or lunches with clients is not the best way to get to know them. Clients see it as product pushing: if it is about you not them. However:

- Dinners where clients can meet other clients are far more welcome.

- Lunches with other clients and outside speakers are again seen to be less about you and more about them.

- An investment club where they meet others and learn about direct investing can be seen as fun.

- Shooting days with other clients.

- Opera with other clients.

- Art evenings with other clients.

I have stressed meeting with other clients because from my experience that is what they like – but not always. Some clients may not want to be seen as a client of yours. You need to know before asking them. This can easily be done by asking them what they would enjoy on the feedback form that you give them with their invoice.

On every occasion that you hold an event for a client, follow up. What did they like about the event and what could you improve? You need to know as much as possible about your clients and then use this knowledge to assist them.

Go at your client's pace, not your pace

You must care for your client in other ways. When you are working for a client, take care to go at their pace, not at the pace you would like to go at. When you are with a small child who has just learned to walk, you do not go marching off looking back with an irritated expression that says, "Why can't you keep up?"

If you want to be a trusted advisor, you need to know and respect where your client is on the learning curve. If they are new into liquid wealth, they are like the toddler and you'll need to take more time explaining and answering their questions. But just as you wouldn't expect a parent to be impatient with a toddler, don't be patronising or impatient with a client. This basic step is often overlooked by advisors who think they are acting in their client's best interests in encouraging them to do things or invest in products for which they are not ready. Take time to nurture and teach them, and they will reward you with trust.

Going at the pace of a client does not mean staying at that pace. Toddlers, like clients, learn and grow. A toddler will grow into a child and from there to a teenager; on occasion, they need and want to be challenged, but it must

be the right challenge at the right time. Providing a good service is an art, but with it comes the right to influence. If used correctly, the client will see this as part of a good service. This influence must be used to good effect to drive up the profits of the business. Do not use it to mis-sell.

Increasing the profits of the business

There are only four ways to increase a business's profits:

- Charge your existing clients more.

- Sell more to your existing clients

- Sell your services and products to new clients.

- Sell new products and services to new clients.

The fourth must be avoided, because it is risky, costly and problematic. The third is what we have been working on in the previous chapters. The first two focus on how to increase profitability from your existing clients.

Charge your existing clients more

Charging your existing clients more is not as simple as putting the price up. Although we have touched upon treating your service or product as a luxury purchase, I do not concur with the view that the more expensive it is, the more highly it will be valued. There is a market price for services as well

as products. You do not want to be the most expensive, but you certainly don't want to be the cheapest. If you simply put up your prices for the same quality of service, some of your existing clients will see your services as too expensive and go elsewhere.

What you need to do is to improve the quality of the service and then you can charge more. A five-star hotel is more expensive than a one-star hotel. Both provide a place to sleep and washing facilities, but the five-star hotel provides a better service and a more luxurious setting. So it should be with the service you provide for your best clients.

On the feedback form that you send to your clients with their invoice, you need to ask how you can improve your service and what they'd be willing to pay for it. Do they want:

- Home visits?

- Extra reporting?

- A dedicated account manager?

- 24/7 service?

- Personal introductions?

- Assistance in working on their goals?

- More time in understanding the advice being given?

As you find out more about what your best clients want and are willing to pay for, you will soon find more ways to assist them as you provide them a better quality service. Asking your clients what they want gives you the opportunity to charge more for the work you are already doing. Service is what the client wants, and in providing better quality service to your best clients, you can charge more.

Remember that a client likes to feel special. Maybe you should think of creating an elite class of client, that get more attention, more privileges and more benefits – which in reality cost you very little but gives you the opportunity to upsell.

Up-selling

Up-selling is when you provide your client with another service or product. Anthony is an immigration and succession lawyer. He has been working for Josh and Melissa on their immigration and tax planning ahead of their arrival into the UK. As they arrive, he sends them a brief note to welcome them and suggests they meet for a celebratory lunch. Over lunch, he asks what arrangements they have in place, should they die while living in the UK and what arrangements they would like to consider. Anthony gives them some case studies showing what he has done for other clients.

It is always easier to up-sell to an existing client than it is to win a new client. The client is already familiar with you and your style of working, so their innate fear of influence from strangers is diminished. They are therefore much more open to new suggestions especially if they are made to feel special; as an existing advisor, you are not seen as pushing product. If you make suggestions, you will be seen as caring for them. The time the client has his or her purse open is the time they are willing to buy more.

Cross-selling

Cross-selling is where you make a referral to someone else in your organisation to provide a service or product. While talking to Josh and Melissa over lunch, Anthony asks them what arrangements they've made for accommodation. They tell him they are currently renting, but are looking to buy. This is a perfect opportunity for Anthony to tell them about his firm's conveyancing department; he gives them John's name as someone he can recommend. He follows up immediately with an email with John's full contact details and makes sure that John is copied in to the email.

To cross-sell well, Anthony needs to know precisely what services and products his organisation can provide and by whom. He needs to know in some detail what their most profitable work is so that he only introduces good quality work to his colleagues. If John is a specialist in property transactions in Mayfair and Chelsea, he will not be best pleased to be referred a client with a one-bedroomed apartment in Ealing.

> If a business is to make the most out of their clients, it must incentivise its staff to cross refer their clients to their colleagues.

It is also imperative that Anthony is rewarded by his organisation for cross- selling, and that any referral must be tracked and attributed to him. If a business is to make the most out of their clients, it must incentivise its staff to cross refer their clients to their colleagues. There needs to be a programme (which should be fun) to help advisors within the organisation discover what colleagues are doing for their clients not only so that cross referring is rewarded, but so that every member of the firm knows what their colleagues are doing and the type of work they want.

Regular sessions of speed networking are ideal to assist with cross referral of business. Advisors from different departments pitch a five-minute case study of what they have done for a specific client (making sure the names, ages and family circumstances are changed to keep the real clients' identity private) to their colleagues across the organisation. Then each member of the audience is asked to vote on whether they have clients who could benefit from this service. Each advisor who has pitched should then be encouraged to publish their case study on an aggregating platform so that his colleagues and clients can be better informed.

Referring new business to your network

Of course, Anthony will not want to stop referring business to Josh and Melissa. In his network are estate agents, interior designers, surveyors and building contractors, all of whom he could refer Josh and Melissa. By making introductions to his network, Anthony will not only win their trust, but he will be able to demonstrate the value of his clients to his network.

Furthermore, if he is successful at referring Josh and Melissa to one or more of his network, they will feel obliged to reciprocate. If they don't, Anthony may decide to remove them from his network, which he can make obvious if he is promoting his news, views and case studies on an aggregating platform.

I often hear advisors saying they don't have clients to whom they can refer business because they are the last in the chain. This is simply not true; if advisors are genuinely caring for their clients as well as their network, they should always be thinking of how they can better serve them by referring them to others in their network. It may seem strange at first, but clients love you to care for their best interests, so it is crazy not to do so consciously and conspicuously.

Lessons can be learned from supermarkets; they are experts in understanding human behaviour. Just because you are a wealth advisor does not mean that buying services is any different from buying food.

How many times does the supermarket appeal to your right brain?

- Buy one get one free. (Logic says: I don't need two)

- Buy while stocks last. (Logic says: I don't need that product)

- Discount applies for a limited period only. (Logic says: I don't particularly want that product)

- 25% extra if you buy now. (Logic says: the extra 25% will probably get thrown away)

- If you buy this product, you may also like this one at half price. (Logic says: I wasn't thinking of getting an extra product)

- Before you leave, what about a sweet treat? (Logic says: It will only make me fat)

Shopping online is even more obvious in its appeal to the right brain. You can't go to the check out without visiting at least three screens of extras to put in your basket – and we have all succumbed. Supermarkets do it because it works. All these calls to action focus on right brain decision-making.

The supermarket knows that once you have your purse open, it's a very small step to tempt you to buy something you wouldn't otherwise have bought. To put it another way, your innate fear is diminished at point of sale, so this is the ideal time to persuade you to buy more. We can see it all around us in retail. When a woman buys shoes, would she like a handbag to go with it? If a man buys a shirt, would he also like a tie?

> Wealth advisors should be aware of these retail selling techniques and use them to their advantage.

Wealth advisors should also be aware of these selling techniques and try to use them to their advantage.

- You have successfully bought your home in the UK. You now need to plan what to do with it if anything were to happen to you.

- As a non-domiciliary and having just completed your tax plan, you may like to know about our succession services.

- As a new customer and having recently inherited on the death of your father, you may like to know more about our charitable planning service. Phone Samantha for your FREE consultation.

- As a valued customer who has spent over £20,000 with us this year, we will charge you half price for the succession plan during the month of June.

There is a school of thought that says luxury goods should not be sold at a discount for fear of damaging the brand. This is true, but there is an exception to this rule. Where the discount is made to an exclusive group of existing customers, then the discount or special offer is seen as a reward for loyalty. Discounts on luxury items should not be seen as a means to increase the customer base. Existing customers do not want to see what they have paid full price for being sold to people who could not otherwise afford them. However, if the discount or special offer is only made to existing customers who have and can afford to pay the full price, then it is seen as a gesture of care. The last example, given above, was a discount to an existing valued customer who had spent a significant sum of money with the organisation already. The discount will be warmly welcomed and will deepen the relationship.

As you start to care for your customers by up-selling and cross-selling, you will need to test what offers and proposals work best by monitoring them and asking for feedback. It will not take long before up-selling and cross- selling start to build a strong brand for your organisation.

Brand building

There are numerous agencies that assist in building brands. Not all are successful. I am reminded about the launch of the British Airways rebranding where the planes had brightly coloured tails which were supposed to show how BA covered the globe. Mrs Thatcher, as she was then, simply placed her scarf over the tail. What was wrong with being proud to be British? They subsequently switched the tails back to the Union Jack.

Branding is not just about colours, typeface, letterheads, logos and straplines. A brand is the personality of a business.

Personality can only really be changed from within. Rather than focus on their brand as if it was something that could be changed by a clever advert or strapline, wealth advisors need to think first about developing the right attributes towards their clients before distilling them into a slogan.

A branding expert cannot turn an Ugly Sister into Cinderella by telling the world she is beautiful.

Prince Charming simply won't fall for her. Wealth advisors need first to ensure that they have the right attributes before calling in the branding experts to point out clearly and honestly that this is Cinderella and not an Ugly Sister trying to shove a fat foot into a dainty slipper. When Prince Charming comes to visit, he will see that what is being said about Cinderella is true and that will make him feel even better. However, if he hears an Ugly Sister being extolled as if she were Cinderella, he'll be annoyed and irritated to find out that he has been misled. People don't like being deceived or treated as if they were stupid.

> A branding expert cannot change an Ugly Sister into Cinderella by telling the world she is beautiful.

It's not easy to develop the right attributes because everyone is resistant to change. This resistance is another form of our innate fear of being influenced by strangers. To learn how to change behaviour, we need to go back to thinking about how we bypassed our innate fear of product pushing:

- Education.

- Aggregation.

- Reciprocation.

- Case studies.

How can we use these to influence the advisors in an organisation to adopt new habits?

Education

At this point, it is worth making the distinction again between education and training. Education is enjoyable because I am finding out things that are interesting and of use to me. Training is what you want me to learn and is of importance to you.

If you are going to educate your staff, it has to be seen as benefiting them first and the organisation only second. What will be of most interest to your advisors is how they can win more business and make more money, but they'll be wary of anything you suggest at first because they'll see it as training, not education. I believe education needs to be introduced subtly.

Although you can probably think of other ways, here is one suggestion. Pick your best advisors and educate them on how to win new business, cross-sell and up-sell. They should be told they are handpicked and are the pioneers. You want to learn with them about how to improve their bonuses and the profitability of the firm. You also want their feedback on the plan before it is rolled out to the rest of the organisation. Each one needs to be educated so they can:

- Identify which is their most profitable work and who are their most profitable clients.

- Plan on how to win new business.

- Manage their time well.

- Use marketing efficiently and effectively.

- Sell.

- Up-sell and cross-sell.

- Build trust.

The education programme must be designed to enable each of them to take each step for themselves, with the aim of winning more business and a bigger bonus.

Aggregation

You then need to aggregate the results and promote them in a manner that encourages other members of staff to want to learn how to win new business. This can be done through an internal newsletter.

Now monitor the education programme's success – and that success needs to be measurable. Introduce regular appraisals where you go through the results and monitor them against the lessons learned. Developing new ways of doing things needs continual reminders, feedback and repetition until better habits are developed.

Reciprocation

You could also introduce some competition and a super-bonus system. The advisor who is in the top three for winning new business for each quarter gets 25% extra bonus for that month.

Applaud your winners, interview them and ask what they will be spending their winnings on, make you as their employer look human, showing that you care.

Case studies

Each new business won or referred can be shared with the whole firm as a case study; this will make the newsletter more readable and at the same time it teaches everyone in

As a culture of care takes hold, not only will profitability rise, but the firm will become a joy to work for.

the organisation what everyone else is doing and for whom, which will encourage and enhance cross-selling.

These newsletters could be published without the private details of winners and extra bonuses and put on an aggregation platform as well as being left in the reception area for prospective clients.

As a culture of care takes hold, not only will profitability rise, but the firm will become a joy to work for. Clients will know that they're being cared for and this positive attitude will become contagious. Only at this point is it time to call in the brand experts. Now their job will not be about disguising an Ugly Sister as Cinderella, but rather turning Cinderella into a princess.

Now you know how to maintain and retain, you need now to build trust, which we cover in the next chapter.

Chapter 8
The Trusted Advisor: building a trusted relationship

Chapter summary:

- Building a trusted relationship.

- Advice is a distressed purchase.

- Four types of problem and how to deal with them.

- Treat your clients as humans and show you're human too.

- What your clients really want.

The benefits of a trusted relationship

There are obvious commercial advantages to having a trusted relationship with your clients. Here are some of them:

- Your bills are paid in full and on time.

- You get repeat business.

- You get referred work from friends and contacts.

- You do not need to go through time-wasting procedures such as proposals, presentations, and long billing narratives.

- The clients are more prepared to do what you propose once understood, without time-wasting justification.

- You save time on learning about the client and their idiosyncrasies.

- You know what their goals are.

I had been working with a client for several years. We'd spent days on end holed up in meeting rooms. I understood what was required and worked tirelessly to do what he wanted. Some three months after the work had been completed, he phoned to ask my opinion on a litigation matter. I said it was not my area of expertise, but would find out the facts, take advice from an expert and come back to him, which I did. He instructed my contact without even meeting him or finding out what his fees were. I asked him why he was prepared to instruct a stranger so quickly. "Garnham," he always called me by my surname, "don't screw up." He said it with a twinkle in his eye and of course I didn't, I cared for him. My contact was delighted with the referral and referred one of his clients to me in return.

How to win trust

As I said in part one, trust needs to be earned through small steps. It boils down to caring for your client. To build trust, the focus needs to be on the client, not the advisor. It needs to be about giving, not getting, but do not be misled. There are a lot of advisors who have a great rapport with their clients, yet delay putting in their fees or chasing for payment.

Caring is when you tell your client what your fees will be and when and how you want to be paid, and then sticking to what you've told them. You do not earn respect or build trust by putting in a fee after the work has been done, when there was no letter of engagement or contract signed. Advisors must learn to be commercial, which means first and foremost recognising the value of your knowledge and expertise and treating it as worth a lot to your client. Peace of mind is extremely valuable for a client and they need to understand that they have to pay for it. Advisors should not therefore rush into giving advice without properly discussing with the client what it is they want, and what it will cost them.

Once the fee arrangement is properly understood, and agreed, advisors then need to understand that building trust is like building any other relationship and involves left brain activity as well as right brain activity.

Trust is not a left brain activity

If I phone my banker, John, to ask for a transfer to my son, he will ask, "Will that be to Edward?" Of course, he can see on the screen in front of him that I have a son called Edward, but I feel good when he mentions my son's name. This is right brain activity and is of great importance in building trust.

A few years ago, I needed a mortgage and John was my first port of call. However, the mortgage rate they quoted was very high. At this point, left brain activity kicked in. I went to the banker with whom I had an existing mortgage, Susy. I did not know Susy well and so was much more reticent and suspicious. This was my innate fear of the influence of strangers popping up. Susy openly said that she could not assist, but introduced me to Peter in another bank, who could. This openness and lack of self-interest made me warm to Suzy and she went up in my estimation – right brain activity. Not only did Peter give me an excellent rate and service, but we ended up working on several other projects together.

Let's go back to John. If the mortgage rate had been higher, but by not much, I would have stayed with him because I trusted him: he knew the names of my children and made me feel good, but the rate was more than twice that charged by Peter. I felt they were using a friendly service to overcharge me and that made me suspicious. Where else were they overcharging me? In this case, my trust in John diminished.

Dan sold his business and was taken to lunch by his bankers. He invested in one of their funds and arranged for them to be his executors. A little later, it was pointed out to him the fees the bank was earning on his fund and the fees they could earn being executor of his will. He immediately cooled. He felt he had been taken advantage of. In due course, he took all his business, which was considerable, away from that bank.

By trying to charge too much for some low hanging fruit, these bankers lost the tree. What they should have done was to give him their best and most reasonably priced service or product and pointed out what good value it was, but it was too tempting to sell him the products that earned them the most in fees, and thereby they lost the client.

Trust is building a relationship

Like any human relationship, left brain and right brain activity ebbs and flows, but there are some basic principles to building a trusted relationship:

- It grows, it doesn't magically pop up.

- It is human, which means it has right brain and left brain characteristics.

- It involves two parties which are not equal.

It grows.

As Chapter 4 pointed out, there is an innate fear of the influence of strangers in us all, and therefore trust has to be planted and nurtured; it won't appear magically. Of course, there is always the 1-3% exception to the rule; some people say they fell in love at first sight and others say, "I knew I could trust him from the moment I saw him". From my experience, I would be cautious of intuition. If it were that reliable, there would not be so many people conned, mis-sold, defrauded, deceived or stolen from. Building trust should be like lighting a fire; it should be slow to catch, gently tended in the initial stages, and, once alight, stoked on a regular basis.

It is human with left and right brain characteristics.

The majority of advisors are obsessed with their area of expertise, and convinced that the reason why they have clients is because of their experience and knowledge. This is further encouraged by their regulatory body, which demands that advisors keep up to date with Continuing Development Points.

Most advisors are of the view that clients are logical and rational and take their advice because of their expertise and knowledge. In fact, most clients expect advisors to have technical competence. What they look for in an advisor is someone who cares and is interested in them. They are looking for someone who understands them, can remember their personal details and tries wherever possible to assist them. These are all right brain characteristics. Remember I only left John, my first banker, because of left brain activity; my inclination was to stay with him. However, as soon as my left brain gained dominance over my right brain, my right brain caught up. I am now far more suspicious of John.

It involves two parties which are not equal.

If we were all rational, and could be persuaded only on the facts, then we would buy on features and not benefits. Cold calling is not hugely effective to begin with, regardless of what is being offered and how relevant it is, but with persistence a relationship can be built up. At this point, the advisor is in a superior position because of his or her knowledge.

With that knowledge and with the use of information gleaned from the relationship, they can start to convey concerns or set out opportunities that the client or prospect may not have thought of. If what is being suggested is of genuine benefit to the client or prospect, then there may be a sale.

An advisor must not use his or her superior knowledge to persuade a client to do something that is not in their best interests, regardless of how much closer it gets him to his own goals.

Taking advice is a distressed purchase

When taking advice, a client is putting themselves in a vulnerable position; they're someone who doesn't know the answer. They may even be a little unclear about the question and will not know how to proceed. This is a distressed purchase. In their normal everyday lives, the UHNW individual, especially if they have been successful, is confident, has authority, and is respected. They **do not like taking advice;** they feel foolish, which is not a nice experience.

Full of knowledge and expertise, the advisor is often tempted to indulge in this superiority and make his client squirm with jargon, complications, time constraints, and further worries. I have seen this used often. A case, for example, that could easily have been wrapped up in four weeks, was spun out for over a year at vast expense, with convoluted explanations and numerous letters and invoices.

This advisor will pick up his bonus at the end of the year and dazzle his professional intermediaries with his expertise and knowledge. Personally, I think this type of advisor is a relic from pre-2008. They do not care for their clients. A culture of greed was the culture we saw being exercised in the build-up to the collapse of Lehman Brothers.

> An advisor should take the burden of responsibility off their clients' shoulders and make what is complicated simple...

The job of an advisor is to take the burden of responsibility off the shoulders of their clients and make what is complicated simple, so that they can take decisions in the light of what they've been told. Nothing should be rushed.

This is a dangerous ploy to cut out left brain activity. The type of advisor who does not want his client to understand the problem is not caring for his client. He is telling his client that he is too stupid to understand the complexities and therefore should trust blindly. A foolish thing to do. In a culture of care, the advisor should take time to explain the issues in a way the client can understand so that the client can make the decisions and be in control. After all, it is the client's money, not the advisor's.

Four types of problem and their solutions

There are four different types of problems. Knowing what type of problem you are encountering will help you manage your clients' expectations in finding a solution.

They are as follows:

1. **Paint by numbers**. When you know the process and the outcome.

2. **Directional**. When you know the process, but not the outcome.

3. **Goal-oriented**. When you know the outcome, but not the process.

4. **Fog.** When you know neither the process nor the outcome.

1. Paint by numbers

An example of this would be registering a trademark. Ed wants to register his company's name, Keep Hush, as a trademark. He knows that it is available for the sectors he wants and so he fills out the forms and registers it.

Paint by numbers problems are easy for advisors to deal with because they can clearly point out what will be achieved, by when, and at what cost. With a paint by numbers type of problem, the advisor can be confident and manage the client's expectations within carefully defined parameters.

2. Directional

An example of this would be mediation of a dispute. Martin has a dispute with Tom about a contract for the purchase of a company. Both Martin and Tom have agreed to mediate their dispute. They both know the process, but neither will know the outcome. If Tom has a good lawyer, he will know what his chances of winning are, but Martin also has a lawyer, and he also thinks he has a good chance of winning.

> An advisor faced with a directional problem needs to explain to the client what to expect in terms of the process, but also to manage their expectations about the outcome.

An advisor faced with a directional problem needs to explain to the client what to expect in terms of the process, but also to manage their expectations as to the unpredictable nature of the outcome. The advisor can explain how much it will cost and the benefits, which will vary according to the outcome. The client can then decide whether they want to proceed, given the costs and uncertainty.

3. Goal-oriented

An example of this would be the announcement in the budget of a new relief for business entrepreneurs which is available if you meet five criteria. Simon meets the five criteria, but will not know how to obtain the relief until the details are known and he seeks advice.

The advisor in this case can manage the client's expectations about the outcome, but cannot give any guide as to how much it is going to cost in getting there, because there is no way of knowing what needs to be done to achieve the known outcome. In a goal-oriented problem, the process must be broken down into individual steps, and reports given at regular intervals to manage expectations along the journey.

4. Fog

Here's an example of a fog. Ann is going to live in France and needs to find out about French laws of succession on her existing home in the UK, her home in France and her business interests in Switzerland. This would be a fog: until she starts the process, she and her lawyers are unlikely to know either the process or the outcome.

Another example would be a conveyance of a property. Let's take Margaret and Bob. They are looking for an apartment in which to live in London; they have found a lovely property and the price looks about right. However, until they have a surveyor's report, do the searches, research some comparables and look at the lease, they will not know whether it is overpriced, what problems they may encounter and whether they will buy it or not.

Another example of a fog is a liquidity event. Basil sells his business for £260 million; he repays his mortgage, buys a new house and then starts thinking about how to invest his money.

An advisor dealing with a fog needs to tell the client clearly that he cannot give any indication about the outcome or the process as to how to get there, which will mean no indication as to costs, time or outcome. In a situation like this, the advisor needs to report often and to manage expectations as to short horizons, making sure to get feedback every step of the way.

An advisor dealing with a fog needs to be aware about how stressful this problem is to the client.

General tips on giving advice

In the course of solving a problem for a client, an advisor may start out thinking that it will be a paint by numbers scenario, but in the course of resolving it he may find it switches to a directional or goal orientation problem or even a fog, and vice versa.

> The moment a problem switches from one type to another, the advisor needs to communicate with his client.

If the problem is a paint by numbers problem, the advisor would have told his client what to expect and how much it will cost. The moment the problem switches, he or she needs to communicate what has cropped up and why the resolution to the problem has changed.

Let's take the example of a house decoration. Benjamin is a builder and decorator and he has been asked to paint and decorate Judith's house. He quotes on the basis of what he can see and has surveyed. However, as he starts work, he lifts up the floorboards and sees subsidence. He immediately stops work and calls Judith to report what he has seen and to communicate to her what would happen if he continued with the painting and decorating without first resolving the subsidence.

Judith is committed to a bill for the painting and decorating of her house; she is certainly not expecting subsidence. If she does not know Benjamin well, she may resist his assessment of the case and ask for a second opinion. Benjamin is frustrated; he cannot proceed without Judith's consent. He is clearly giving her good advice, but she sees it as a product push, the innate fear of being influenced by a stranger is triggered and she resists what Benjamin is telling her. Benjamin should communicate what he's discovered in a sensitive manner. He could offer to get Judith a second opinion, for example. He needs to be sympathetic to how she will react; maybe he could offer her a discount on the painting and decorating. He would be foolish to go back to Judith with, "Guess what we've discovered, a problem that will double your bill!" Naturally, she will not react well.

Putting this in the context of a professional advisor, some clients may be slow at understanding complex issues, and may not be aligned with what you would like them to do, but you must always remember that they are paying you to give advice, and it should be the client who makes the decisions.

Stephen is advising Marcos who is a non-domiciled person (which means his father was born and brought up outside the UK), on becoming UK resident. He advises that to take advantage of the favourable non-dom remittance basis of tax (which means he need only pay tax on the income and gains he makes in the UK or brings into the UK), that Marcos will need to pay an annual fee of £30,000 in due course, and will need to be very careful as to what monies he brings into the country. Marcos may decide that he does not want the hassle of the restrictions of being a non-dom and he would prefer to be taxed on his worldwide income and gains as if he were a UK domiciliary.

Stephen may be tempted to tell him at this stage not to be so daft, but it is not Stephen's call: it is his client's decision that counts. Marcos may alternatively suggest that he won't pay the annual fee or report on his worldwide income and gains because HMRC will never find out. Stephen, at this point, must tell Marcos that this is breaking the law and it is not acceptable. He needs to explain the consequences of non-disclosure, which could include a full blown tax investigation with tax, penalties and interest to be paid on unpaid income and gains. He will also need to tell Marcos that HMRC has extensive powers to find information from other jurisdictions, and that it is foolish in the extreme to evade tax. Paying all taxes due gives peace of mind, which any advisor who cares knows is priceless.

Professionals think they know best

Jane is doing a probate for Justin whose father died recently. Justin sends Jane a list of his father's assets and the first thing that catches her eye is a house and boat in Sardinia. She drops what she is doing to talk to a colleague who has had experience in dealing with Italian situs assets in a probate. He puts down some time on Justin's matter. Then she asks her assistant to research the succession laws in Italy for real estate and moveables. Only after considerable work has been done does she go back to discuss the house and boat in Italy with Justin. She did not want to go back to Justin until she was confident about how to tackle the probate of the Italian assets, which took her considerable time and effort.

This is the equivalent of Benjamin starting to survey the extent of the work to repair the subsidence before discussing it with Judith, and then charging her for the work done, without her consent for him to carry it out. Judith would be well within her contractual rights to refuse to pay Benjamin. She could choose another firm to do the subsidence work, because it is not within her contract with Benjamin.

However, Jane feels uncomfortable going back to Justin without knowing what needs to be done with the Italian assets in his estate, so she does the work without discussing it with her client. She may not know the first thing about the succession rules of Italian situs assets, and indeed may not be the best person to handle this aspect of the probate.

Most professional advisors don't like feeling uncomfortable, or not knowing how to fix a problem. They have a tendency to start resolving a problem before discussing it with clients. Advisors see themselves as problem fixers and worry that clients will go elsewhere if they find out that there are gaps in their knowledge.

> Professional advisors are secretly fearful of their clients. They don't like people who are unpredictable or slow to understand.

The moment Jane sees Italian assets in the estate, rather than going to see a colleague and starting the work, she should pick up the phone to Justin and tell him that the Italian assets could complicate the probate. She should then ask her client whether his father had taken advice with regard to the succession of the house and the boat. Justin will rummage through his father's papers for the requisite advice, and may indeed find some very helpful information which could help Jane, save Justin on costs, and enable them to work together.

Professional advisors are secretly fearful of their clients. They don't like people who behave irrationally, are unpredictable and slow to understand.

Advisors are far more comfortable with the certainty and logic of their area of expertise. It is a lot easier to treat their clients like foolish children, ramming what is good for them down their throats like medicine for a disease they are too young and foolish to understand.

But clients do not like being treated like foolish children and if they are, they will pay their bills late and negotiate down their fees. Advisors who treat their clients like this do not get repeat business, and work is rarely referred to them.

Professional advisors have spent years observing their colleagues treating their clients like children and have copied them. Very few advisors will have been given any training on how to win and retain new business, other than cold calling, and simply know no other way. If advisors find it hard to change, then their clients need to teach them by simply demanding a better service, terminating relationships that do not serve them, and switching to advisors who adopt a culture of care.

Professional advisors also need to remind themselves of the law of contract, and if advisors forget their clients need to remind them. Clients should not sign nonspecific letters of engagement and should not pay for anything about which they do not know in advance.

Advisors who are paid late unwittingly, and probably inadvertently, have an attitude that says, "I know what is best for you. So do as I say and pay me what I ask". A culture of care, on the other hand, asks, "What are you trying to achieve? Let's work on this together," and, "I may not be the best person to help you on this, but I know someone who is". This attitude gets bills paid on time and in full. In addition, the people to whom you refer business will refer business back to you.

Don't be afraid to ask

Marvin is a new young advisor to the inner circle of a UHNW individual. He is invited to his first meeting of advisors. At one point, Rachel, an advisor to the family for many years, says, "Don't forget the Clause Five complications". Everyone in the room laughs and nods their heads. Marvin doesn't know what the Clause

> Caring for clients means caring less about knowing it all – it is simply not possible for you to know everything.

Five complications are, and does not know whether to say so or not. He's nervous, so he lets it pass. Then Greg retorts, "It's a repeat of 2004 and as if Clause Five never happened." Everyone nods and laughs again. Now what is Marvin to do? Admit that he let the first mention of Clause Five pass and that he doesn't know what the reference to 2004 is about either?

As Marvin worries about looking foolish and not knowing what they are talking about, he loses focus and is unable to give 100% to the issues at hand. The other advisors wonder whether he will add any value to their board.

If, however, Marvin had said, "I'm sorry but I'm not fully up to speed on the Clause Five issue. Could someone explain?" Rachel would have been delighted to explain and Greg would probably have explained the 2004 reference as well, without being asked.

Caring for clients means caring less about knowing it all – it is simply not possible for you to know everything. Furthermore, trust will not be diminished by admitting to a lack of knowledge. In fact, it may enhance trust because the advisor is seen as honest, keen to learn, and human.

Clients are human – treat them as such

The other trap professional advisors fall into when they think of themselves as problem fixers rather than advisors who care for their clients is that as soon as the problem is fixed, they don't contact their clients again. Clients who have worked closely with an advisor over a period of time feel let down; as if they've been treated like an ATM. Once the advisor has been paid, he moves on to another problem and another fee.

The client, however, has vested time, money and effort in resolving a problem and has started to trust his or her advisor. They don't want client lunches and dinners, they do not want to be romanced; they just want to be treated as a human being. They want their advisors to **continue to care**.

Most advisors could share some knowledge from their network with a client with a little note saying, "I thought you may be interested in this". It is not a product push, it reminds the client that their advisor is still thinking about them, and keeps the relationship alive. As and when a problem arises, the clients will not hesitate to come back. It's so simple and yet so few advisors do it. Clients are human: if you want to build trust and win new business, treat them as such.

Practical ways to build trust with a client

- **Involve the client in the process.** In the example above, Jane asked Justin if his father had taken advice with regard to the house in Italy; this involves the client and they like that. No client likes to be made to feel like a foolish child who is too stupid to understand what the issues are.

- **Admitting gaps in the advisor's knowledge** makes a client feel less foolish and encourages him or her to ask questions. If a client does not understand a complex issue, the advisor should say, "I'm probably not explaining it very well". This will probably be the case!

- **Don't leave common sense outside your office door.** If you are giving advice on capital gains tax, find out if the client has made a gain, and before advising on inheritance tax, ask what the client wants to do with their wealth on death. If it is to give it all away to charity before death, then the advice may be significantly different.

- **Ask the client how often they want reports**, in what format and how much detail. This should be fed into the billing process, but the client will feel good that his or her advisor has not just assumed what sort of reports, format and frequency they want; they bothered to ask.

- **Make meetings more meaningful**, with an agenda and goals, sending out all the material that needs to be discussed ahead of the meeting. Make sure that everyone who needs to be at the meeting is there, and follow up to ask for feedback and minutes.

- **Being accessible**; answer all calls within 24 hours. If you are in a meeting, your voicemail should say so and when you are likely to return. It should also give the name of someone else they can contact if the matter is urgent.

- **Stick to times and dates**; in particular deadlines. Wasting someone's time, whoever it is, is a sign of disrespect.

What does the client want from his advisor?

A client wants his advisor to show that he or she cares, by:

- **Knowing about their business**. Set up Google alerts so that you know what is going on with their business.

- **Keeping up to date with them and their family**. Make sure you are up- to-date with what they are doing.

- **Sharing information they may need from your network**. It shows you care.

- **Engaging in non-business activities**. Personalise your engagement with them.

- **Trying to engage in their wider interests**. By getting to know more about them not only do you show you care, but you'll also know exactly what expertise to share from your network.

- **Trying wherever and whenever possible to be helpful and show you care.**

- **Bringing them new ideas**. They want to build a relationship with their advisors, and advisors must do what they can to encourage that at all times.

A trusted relationship

Being an advisor to an UHNW individual, especially those who have overcome adversity and disappointment to be a success, is a privilege and an honour. The fact that these people want to trust you and to build up a relationship with you beyond the client/advisor role, is a surprise for some advisors. Embrace the opportunity – it can be hugely rewarding, fun and enriching.

Building a trusted relationship is essentially about building client relationships based on trust. Treat your clients as human beings; they do not just want your advice, they want to see that you care. When you do, the work will increase and the rewards will be much more than financial; they will be deep and meaningful. Enjoy!

If you would like to know more, about how to build trusted relationships simply scan the code or copy the link **http://www.garnhamfos.com/wbfpc-extras/chapter-8-training-material** for some training material which will assist you.

Book Extras

We want you to get the most out of each of the Eight Chapters of this book *'Uncovering the Secrets of Winning Business from Private Clients'*, which is why we have prepared educational videos, helpful accompanying notes and questionnaires for most Chapters.

If you wish to buy all and get one FREE,
simply access through scanning the code below or copy the link
**http://www.garnhamfos.com/wbfpc-extras/
chapters-1-8-training-materials**

Turn to page 143 if you want to see how the accompanying notes and questionnaires can get you started in building a Ring of Confidence for your clients using your close network of advisers.

BConnect Club

Join our Exclusive Club for UHNW families where they can access your relevant information, luxury products and amazing private deals launched in October 2017. BConnect Club not only puts you directly in front of your target market either offline or online – but also gives you the tools you need to network efficiently and effectively with your closest and most relevant contacts.

Scan the code below or copy the link
http://www.bconnectclub.com